Department of the Environment
Ancient Monuments and Historic Building

GU01018296

Fountains Abbey

NORTH YORKSHIRE

R. GILYARD-BEER OBE, MA, FSA
Formerly Assistant Chief Inspector of Ancient Monuments

LONDON: HER MAJESTY'S STATIONERY OFFICE

ISBN 0 11 670125 0

Contents

KEY TO THE PLANS

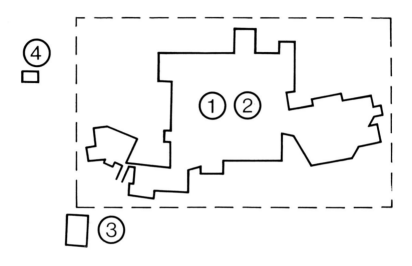

Plan 1   Ground floor of the abbey (*at end of guide*)
Plan 2   First floor of the abbey (*at end of guide*)
Plan 3   Bakehouse and Malthouse (*page 76*)
Plan 4   Gatehouse of the Great Court (*page 73*)

Plan of the abbey precincts (*pages 40-1*)

Key to the dating can be found on Plan 1 at the end of the guide

History

The early years, 1132–35

In the summer of 1132 the Benedictine abbey of St Mary at York was half a century old. Wealthy and powerful, its reputation stood high, but its monks had settled down to an easy way of life, adopting the relaxations of diet and dress that were common to most of the older houses of black monks. To a small section of the convent this savoured of backsliding, and six of them, guided by Richard the sacrist of the abbey, began to discuss together their common desire for a life of greater austerity. The sacrist was a man to inspire others but not to lead them, so they sought the advice of their prior, another and very different Richard, practical, wise, and a friend of Archbishop Thurstan of York. They found that the prior shared their views and was prepared to put their case to the abbot.

Abbot Geoffrey of York was then an old man, well-meaning but set in his ways. He regarded the prior's views as tantamount to apostasy, and thought it intolerable that a small group of his monks should bring scandal on the abbey by wishing to declare a law unto themselves. Discussions dragged on into the autumn with nothing settled, whilst the number of dissident monks grew to thirteen and now included the prior, subprior, sacrist, precentor, and almoner. Finally Prior Richard, despairing of a solution, took his case over the abbot's head to the archbishop and, with Thurstan's decision to make a visitation of the abbey, any remaining hope of a compromise was at an end. The abbot gathered together representatives of other Benedictine and Cluniac houses to strengthen his hand, and when the archbishop arrived there was a brawl in the cloister as these black monks tried to prevent his officials from entering the chapter house. In the midst of uproar, Thurstan placed the abbey under an interdict and shepherded the thirteen dissenters into the church, barring the door for fear of violence.

From the church he led them to his palace where they stayed through October and November, until he took them with him to celebrate Christmas at his collegiate church of Ripon. Two days later, on 27 December 1132, he led them from Ripon to some waste land three miles to the west in the narrow valley of the little River Skell and there he presided over their establishment as a new and independent convent and over the election of Prior Richard as their first abbot. There were springs of good water in the rocky sides of the valley, and from these they chose to call their new abbey 'Fountains'.

Abbot Richard and his convent now belonged to no recognized Order of monks and, in the depth of winter, possessed only the clothes on their backs, a store of bread given by the archbishop, and the uncultivated land on which they stood. It was a place 'uninhabited for all the centuries back, thick set with thorns, and fit rather to be the lair of wild beasts than the home of human beings'. But the little convent lacked nothing in zeal and resolution; no fewer than eight of its thirteen members were eventually to become abbots, and one was to become a saint. The bitter winter was spent sheltering first under the rocks and then under a great elm whilst they built a hut and a chapel and cleared land for a garden.

When the winter was over they decided to seek adoption by the Cistercian Order, newly planted in the north at Rievaulx in 1131, for the life advocated by it and by the Order of Savigny had influenced them deeply when they were still at York. Their petition was accepted, their abbey was received as a daughter-house by Clairvaux in Burgundy, and Geoffrey d'Ainai, an experienced monk of Clairvaux, returned with their messengers to Fountains to teach the new convent the Cistercian way of life.

Nevertheless the new foundation attracted no outside support and, as the archbishop's endowment was insufficient, the monks came near to starvation on more than one occasion during their first years in Skelldale, at one time being reduced to living on gruel made from elm leaves. By 1135 the position was so desperate that Abbot Richard crossed to Clairvaux to ask permission for the convent to leave England. St Bernard, abbot of Clairvaux, agreed and set aside his abbey's grange of Longué as a home for them. This proved unnecessary in the event, for when Richard returned to Fountains he found that Hugh, dean of York, had retired to end his days at the abbey, bringing with him his library and considerable wealth. His example was followed by Serlo and Tosti, canons of York, and Fountains at last had a reasonable financial provision.

Years of growth, 1135–1203

Secure in the knowledge that their benefactions would now go to an enduring institution, and stimulated by the convent's growing reputation for strict religious observance, local lords and the great northern families of Mowbray, Percy, Romelli, and the earls of Richmond began to make extensive grants of land to the abbey, and this stream of benefactions continued for almost a century.

Meanwhile the numbers of the convent grew rapidly, a start was made on the construction of permanent buildings, and between January 1138 and February 1139 colonies of monks set out from Fountains to found new abbeys at Newminster in Northumberland and at Kirkstead and Louth Park in Lincolnshire. Abbot Richard's reputation grew with that of his convent. The Papal Legate Alberic was so impressed with his qualities that he decided to take him to Rome, and Richard was appointed Archbishop Thurstan's delegate to the Lateran Council. But on his arrival in Italy the abbot contracted fever, and he died there in April 1139.

His unwilling successor as second abbot was his namesake Richard, prior of Fountains and once sacrist of York, an unworldly and retiring man who shrank from the administrative duties imposed on him by his office and who suffered from a nervous stammer when speaking in public. On his annual journeys to the General Chapter of the Order he repeatedly begged St Bernard to release him from the abbacy, but his monks would not hear of this, prizing his intense religious conviction and his outstanding gift of resolving their spiritual problems.

It was the misfortune of this shy man to involve Fountains in a damaging public controversy over the succession to the see of York. Archbishop Thurstan died in 1140 and King Stephen procured the election of William Fitzherbert to the archbishopric. The Augustinians and Cistercians were strongly opposed to this and, with the aid of St Bernard and on the strength of evidence given by Abbot Richard II in Rome, they managed to persuade the pope to withhold recognition of the election. In the midst of this controversy Abbot Richard II died when visiting Clairvaux. St Bernard, having in mind that Fountains had now earned the enmity of the king and had lost its patron the archbishop and both the guiding spirits of the secession from York, intervened to provide the abbey with a strong head.

Henry Murdac, abbot of Vauclair, was sent to England ostensibly to advise the convent in the election of a new abbot, but actually to be elected abbot himself in 1144. A Yorkshireman and a friend of St Bernard, he was a zealot forceful to the point of being overbearing. As the first abbot of Fountains to have been trained in continental Cistercian practice he set about reforming the abbey and rooting out the last remnants of Benedictine custom that lingered from the old

7

days at York. Under his rule the convent continued to grow in numbers and reputation, and colonies were sent out to found new daughter-houses at Woburn in Bedfordshire, at Kirkstall in Yorkshire, at Vaudey in Lincolnshire, and over the sea to Lysekloster in Norway between 1145 and 1147.

Abbot Murdac threw himself into the attack on William Fitzherbert with energy, bringing accusations against him at the Council of Reims that led to the archbishop's deposition in 1147. Fitzherbert's supporters were not slow to retaliate. They marched on Fountains with the intention of killing the abbot and, failing to find him, sacked the buildings and set fire to them. Later that year Murdac was himself elected archbishop of York, but the king refused to invest him with the temporalities of the see and feeling in York ran so high against him that he took up residence in Ripon.

Circumstances compelled Archbishop Henry to remain at Ripon from 1147 to 1151, and throughout these years he continued to impose his will on Fountains, treating the abbots elected in his stead as no more than deputies. The first was Abbot Maurice, a scholar of repute who had been subprior of Durham before joining the Cistercian Order and becoming second abbot of Rievaulx and then abbot of Fountains. In three months Abbot Maurice had decided that his position at Fountains was intolerable and had retired to Rievaulx, to be succeeded by Thorold, another learned monk of that abbey. Abbot Thorold ruled until 1150, but he was too independent for the domineering archbishop's liking and St Bernard removed him from office. He retired to Rievaulx and eventually became abbot of Trois-Fontaines in Champagne.

Once again St Bernard felt it necessary to intervene in order to provide Fountains with an abbot capable of handling the situation, and his choice was an astute one. Abbot Richard III, elected in 1150, was a native of York who had become a monk at Clairvaux and had been precentor there and abbot of Vauclair. He was a man of austere life who had been a personal friend of Archbishop Henry in France and who was tactful enough to keep the peace with him until the archbishop died in 1153. After this, a reconciliation was arranged between the abbey and the restored Archbishop William, ending the quarrel that had disturbed and weakened Fountains for thirteen years.

The disturbances had left their mark internally as well as externally. In his early years, Abbot Richard III was faced with dissension amongst

his monks and had to go to the length of expelling those he took to be the ringleaders of the opposition. He ruled for twenty years, and by the time of his death Fountains, Byland, and Rievaulx had come to be regarded as the three 'shining lights' of the Order in England. In his time the abbey sent out a colony to found its eighth and last daughter-house at Meaux in East Yorkshire.

Robert, formerly abbot of Pipewell, succeeded in 1170, and showed himself to be a capable administrator who ruled firmly and well, leaving behind a name for hospitality to rich and poor alike. He was followed in 1180 by the last of the old school of zealots, Abbot

William, who had left the Augustinians of Gisborough to join the Cistercians under St Robert of Newminster and had risen to be abbot of that house. He came to Fountains already an old man wasted by continual austerities, and the brethren feared that he might not have the strength to carry out his duties. The fear proved groundless, for he governed well and vigorously through wisely chosen subordinates, and when in 1190 he was laid to rest in the chapter house it was remembered of him that he had ruled with gentleness.

After this succession of energetic administrators, Fountains could afford an abbot distinguished more for his grasp of spiritual than temporal matters. Abbot Ralph Haget came of a good landed northern family and had been a soldier in his youth. He entered Fountains partly on the advice of his friend Sinnulph, a lay-brother of the abbey, and partly because of an experience in a village chapel where a voice from the Cross admonished him to change his way of life. He was elected abbot of Fountains after a rough passage of nine years as abbot of Kirkstall, where he showed no great talent for business. But the brethren loved and respected him for his spiritual gifts, his charm and his wit, and during the famine of 1194 he organized a refugee camp for the destitute and starving outside the abbey gates. Nor was his rule without material benefit, for both his father and his brother made important gifts of land to the abbey.

Years of prosperity, 1203–65

When Abbot Haget died in 1203 there had been a continuous flow of benefactions to Fountains for some sixty-five years and, although this was to continue into the thirteenth century, the broad pattern of the abbey's estates was already settled. It was a pattern that owed much to chance, for individual gifts saw to it that the convent held scattered parcels of land in many places, and there were few vills within a radius of ten miles of Ripon that did not contain abbey property. But the early Cistercians were expert agricultural pioneers, and their aim was to consolidate and regularize individual estates to a degree that would enable them to practise high farming.

In this they relied much on the labour force provided by the lay-brothers, the unlettered class of monks that devoted itself to manual labour and that in early times outnumbered the choir-monks who maintained the continuous round of services in the abbey. There is no record of the numbers of lay-brothers at Fountains in the twelfth and thirteenth centuries, but there is every reason to believe that they were comparable with the five or six hundred of contemporary Rievaulx, and that they were quartered partly in the abbey and partly on the granges that formed the focal points of the consolidated estates.

This policy of centralized farming making use of direct monastic labour cut across the traditional agricultural economy of the country-side, and in their single mindedness the early Cistercians did not shrink from evicting the existing population of an estate if it seemed that the land could be better exploited by being 'reduced to a grange'. It was a policy that bred hard feelings and unpopularity, and Fountains is known to have depopulated the hamlets of Cayton, Greenberry, and Thorpe Underwoods in order to create granges.

The seven abbots who followed Abbot Haget and between them ruled from 1203 to 1265 were largely responsible for completing the work of consolidation that had been started in the second half of the twelfth century. It involved soliciting new grants, arranging exchanges of land, and purchasing plots to round off existing holding. As other monasteries were engaged in the same activities it also involved negoti-ating agreements to establish what would today be called 'spheres of influence' in which each monastery could increase its holding without fear of conflict. Fountains entered into more than twenty such agree-ments with fifteen different religious houses, mostly from the time of Abbot Pipewell to that of Abbot Alexander (1170–1265).

The pattern that emerged from this was an impressive one. There were a few isolated granges far from the abbey; Bradley near Hudders-field, an estate of 4,400 acres, was one, and Allerdale in Cumberland another, and for these wayleaves had to be secured to enable stock to be moved back to the abbey. But in general the more distant granges were linked to the mother-house by others at intervals of about ten miles to act as staging-posts. In this way Baldersby served as a stepping stone to Kirby Wiske, which gave access northwards to Cowton out in the Vale of Mowbray, and north-eastwards by way of Busby to Eston in Cleveland and the coast. Similarly, Marton and Thorpe Underwoods were stages on the way to Hammerton, Marston, and York, and so to the important grange of Wheldrake on the Derwent.

But the main landed strength of Fountains lay in the west. Here a formidable array of home granges outside the precinct stretched from Morker, Cayton, and Haddockstanes on the south, through Warsill on the west to Swanley, Galphay and Sutton on the north, Beyond these,

11

exploitation of the land was based on granges set on the floor of the dales. In this way lower Wensleydale was served by Sleningford, and bracketed higher up by Aldburgh and Nutwith. Pott Grange lay on the flank of Colsterdale, and Bramley at the headwaters of the River Laver. Nidderdale, bracketed by Dacre, Heyshaw and Brimham, was served higher up by Bouthwaite. Kilnsey stood in upper Wharfedale, Arncliffe in Littondale, Malham and the two granges of Bordley lay off the head of Airedale, and Arnford was planted in Ribblesdale. The smaller lodges dependent on these granges followed the gills into the very folds of the Pennines at Foxup and Cosh, Upper Hesleden and Fornagill, Lofthouse, Throp and many another site on the edge of the high moors where the names of Fountains Earth and Fountains Fell still bear witness to the abbey's dominant interest in a vast expanse of land stretching almost without a break from its west gates out into Lancashire.

Consolidation was a costly business, and in carrying it out the abbots were looking towards the future benefits of centralized farming. Nor was it the only expense incurred in the first half of the thirteenth century. Abbot John of York had to employ money as well as tact to steer the abbey through the difficult years of King John's enmity towards the Cistercians, and he and his two successors, Abbot John of Hessle who became bishop of Ely, and Abbot John of Kent, were engaged in expensive building works until 1247. These three Johns were followed by Abbot Stephen of Eston, a theologian and writer of some talent, who died on visitation at Vaudey Abbey in 1252 and was buried there, his tomb later being reputed to 'blaze with miracles'.

These abbots and their successors into the second half of the thirteenth century could meet high expenses because Fountains was now one of the most powerful religious houses in the north and the richest of its Order in England. The principal source of its great wealth was wool. All the granges had a basis in mixed farming, but many of them also developed specialized activities. Iron was mined and smelted in Calderdale and Nidderdale, where there were also important lead-mines. Stone and slate were quarried in Craven, Nidderdale, Skelldale and on Hutton Moor, and millstones were worked at Sawley and at Crossland near Huddersfield. Sea-fishing was practised off Teesmouth, and footholds were secured in the fish markets of Redcar and Scarborough. The Swale, the Wiske, the Derwent, and the whole course of the Ure and the Ouse from Boroughbridge to York served for river-fishing, whilst lake-fishing was carried out on Malham Tarn and Derwentwater. Fish-culture was practised on several granges, but principally in some twenty acres of artificial ponds in Fountains Park close to the precinct. Buildings were secured in Boston to act as a headquarters for the abbey's agents during the great fairs of St Botulph, and in York the abbey had its own town house with resident caretaker and cook to look after the officers of the monastery when they were in the city on business.

But the most important and lucrative form of specialization was the growth and sale of wool. Here, with true Cistercian thrift, profitable use was made of the great tracts of waste fells that had been granted to the abbey, and they became sheep-runs controlled from the lodges tucked into the gills of the high moors. Each year the flocks were brought down to lowland granges that acted as shearing-stations, and the clip was transported by cart and by boat to York for sale in bulk. By the end of the thirteenth century Fountains had become the largest producer of wool in the north, with an annual clip implying flocks of more than 15,000 sheep, and its receipts from the sale of wool alone amounted to almost three times its revenue from all other sources.

Crisis and controversy, 1265–1436

Wool brought money, and when money was not handled with skill it could and did bring disaster. Particularly dangerous for the monks was the practice of signing contracts with the great continental firms of merchants for the supply of wool over a period of years against a substantial payment in advance. This provided a standing temptation for the convent to anticipate its real revenue, and when the quantity or quality of the clip fell short of the estimate on which the contract was based the abbey fell into debt. By 1274 Fountains was £900 in debt to the York Jewry, and the king found it necessary to appoint Peter Willoughby as an independent commissioner to take the abbey's finances out of the hands of the convent and to administer them more soundly. He succeeded in paying off the debt, but the lesson was not heeded, for in 1276 Abbot Peter Alyng made Fountains an object of scandal by signing a four-year contract with a firm of Florentine merchants, pledging the abbey itself as security for completion. In 1280 an epidemic of sheep-scab ushered in lean years for the wool growers, and the omission of Abbot Henry Otley and Abbot Robert Thornton from the numeration of the abbots probably bears witness

13

to their inability to cope with the situation. The abbey's debt rose to the catastrophic figure of £6373 and in 1291 the king again had to put in a commissioner, his justice John of Berwick, to try and achieve some measure of financial stability.

With the turn of the century, domestic maladministration was overshadowed by national disaster. For ten years after the English defeat at Bannockburn the north was open to Scottish raids, and the estates of Fountains suffered severely, several granges being reduced to a state bordering on ruin. To this was added the failure of the harvest in 1315, followed by famine, and by 1318 burning and plundering of the estates were making it difficult to raise enough funds to support the convent. Meanwhile, Abbot Walter Coxwold received a spate of instructions for raising men to defend the north, in 1318 and 1321 against

Young Ash Trees.

Windows over the Sellen

Reproduced by kind permission of the Society of Antiquaries

the Scots, and in 1322 against the rebel earl of Lancaster. The spirit of lawlessness promoted by these events went on into the middle of the century, and at the same time the rate of recruitment of the lay-brethren dwindled throughout the Order until they practically ceased to exist as a separate class and Fountains was deprived of its main source of direct labour.

This produced a profound change in the economy of the abbey's estates. Some granges were now run by hired labour under salaried bailiffs. Others, damaged in the wars, were leased to secular tenants by Abbot Coxwold in 1336, and still others converted into vills by Abbot Robert Monkton in 1363, producing a complete reversal of the earlier policy of depopulation. Fountains now began to subsist on rents in money and in kind.

The early years of the fifteenth century saw more trouble for the abbey. In 1384 the scholarly Abbot William Gower went blind in his old age and was succeeded by the forceful Abbot Robert Burley. These were the years of the Papal Schism when the existence of rival popes split the allegiance of the Cistercian Order and led to the creation of an English Chapter, and to opportunities for ambitious monks and laymen to dispute the validity of elections. Abbot Burley was involved in such a dispute at the daughter-house of Meaux where, in 1396, he did not hesitate to deploy archers in front of the gatehouse to prevent the English Chapter from ousting Thomas Burton, his candidate for the abbacy.

Others were not slow to learn from his example. When Abbot Burley died in 1410, the delegates of the English Chapter, failing to get a sufficient number of votes for a successor at Fountains, appointed the monk Roger Frank as abbot. Their action was challenged by Abbot John Ripon of Meaux who put himself forward as a candidate and appealed to the pope. The complex legal struggle between Frank and Ripon lasted for six years and, before it ended, involved not only the English Chapter and the pope, but the Council of Constance, parliament, and the king himself. By 1414 the king had evicted Frank and replaced him by Ripon, but the matter did not end there. Frank and thirteen fugitive monks from Fountains wandered the north disguised in secular clothes, fomenting opposition. His relatives made an attempt to murder Abbot Ripon on the road to London. Tenants on the abbey's estates took sides in the quarrel, and in Craven conditions verged on a minor civil war. In 1423 the abbey was plundered after an attack with scaling-ladders and 1431 the home granges were raided and damaged.

Recovery and dissolution, 1436–1539

After these alarms and excursions, the rest of the fifteenth century proved to be a period of quiet consolidation and modest prosperity. The long and wise rule of the learned Abbot John Greenwell, despite his uncertain health, restored stability to the convent. Its numbers had now dwindled to thirty monks, with 117 servants and workmen, but the abbot was recognized as a great northern potentate and such granges as Brimham, Baldersby and Thorpe Underwoods were converted into country houses for his use. Abbot Greenwell and Abbot

John Darnton, another just and capable administrator, were both Commissaries of the abbot of Cîteaux and Reformers of the Cistercian Order in England.

When Abbot Darnton died in 1495 he was succeeded by Marmaduke Huby, the best known and perhaps the greatest abbot of Fountains. Huby had already been a monk and obedientiary in the abbey for some thirty years when he was elected abbot, and to this long apprenticeship he added outstanding qualities of energy and decision. Although he is mainly remembered today as the builder of the great tower of the abbey church, during his thirty years as abbot he left his mark on practically every aspect of the affairs of his abbey and of his Order. As Reformer of the Cistercians he was described as a venerable father who stood like a golden and unbreakable column in his zeal for the Order, and under him the number of monks at Fountains, once as low as twenty-two, rose to fifty-two. He commissioned a revised inventory of the abbey's title deeds, he was an indefatigable repairer and rebuilder of the abbey's granges and chapels, and he was responsible for putting the Order's College of St Bernard at Oxford on a firm footing.

FA—C

Abbot Huby died in 1526, and by 1530 there were signs that his successor, Abbot William Thirsk, was not a prudent ruler. There is evidence that he was selling abbey timber without consulting the convent, although it would be unwise to place too much reliance on the more picturesque tales of his misdeeds, such as that which represents him taking jewels from the sacristy at dead of night to sell to a Cheapside goldsmith. The events that were the real cause of Abbot Thirsk's downfall started in 1533 when he questioned the authority of Thomas Cromwell, the king's chief minister, over the deposition of the abbot of Rievaulx. This marked him as a man unlikely to be amenable to the king's wishes, and when Dr Layton and Dr Legh, the royal agents for the visitation of the monasteries, arrived at Fountains in 1536, they forced the abbot to resign. Provided with a comfortable pension, he went to stay with his friend Abbot Sedbergh of Jervaulx.

His successor, the 39th and last abbot of Fountains, was Marmaduke Bradley, a monk who had been in disgrace in Abbot Huby's time but had been pardoned by Abbot Guillaume du Boisset of Cîteaux. He had obtained the prebend of Thorpe in Ripon Minster and the mastership of the hospital of St Mary Magdalene there. No doubt the visitors saw in him a politic and pliable man who would suit the king's interests, but in this their judgment proved faulty. Abbot Bradley was certainly politic but by no means pliable and he made it clear that, although he had no illusions about the likely fate of his monastery, he was going to protect its interests whilst it lasted and his own thereafter. He not only refused Cromwell's request that he should give up his prebend, but also resisted attempts to transfer the leases of abbey granges to nominees of the king.

The first year of his rule saw the outbreak of the rising in favour of the monasteries, known as the Pilgrimage of Grace. Abbot Bradley kept Fountains aloof from this, but his predecessor ex-Abbot Thirsk was less fortunate, for one of the incidents in the rising centred on Jervaulx Abbey where he had been staying. Along with his friend Abbot Sedbergh, Thirsk was accused of complicity in the insurrection, imprisoned in the Tower of London, and found guilty of treason at Westminster. In May 1537 he was hanged, drawn and quartered at Tyburn.

The abbey was now near its end. The smaller monasteries had already been suppressed, and in January 1538 a visitation of the greater monasteries was started with the express purpose of procuring their surrender.

It was a long business, and not until 26 November 1539 did the convent of Fountains gather in the chapter house to surrender their abbey and all its possessions to the king. Pensions were assigned two days later, Abbot Bradley receiving a comfortable £100 a year, Prior Thomas Kydde £8, and thirty monks sums varying from £5 to £6 13s. 4d.

The wealth that fell into the king's hands was impressive. Fountains was the richest Cistercian monastery in the British Isles, with a clear annual revenue of over £1000. The inventory of its sacristies reads like a tale of treasure trove; 80 copes amongst a multitude of other vestments, 22 silver chalices, two croziers with silver heads and two mitres encrusted with silver-gilt ornament, reliquaries of St Anne, St Lawrence and the True Cross, and plate amounting to 2840 oz even without the gold ornaments of the high altar.

Whilst the commissioners were disposing of this for the king's profit, ex-Abbot Bradley retired to the prebend at Ripon that he had so wisely refused to surrender, and there he lived on until 1553, a respected member of the chapter noted for his benefactions to the fabric.

After the dissolution

The abbey buildings stood empty but undamaged for a few months because a paper scheme existed to make them the cathedral of a new bishopric with jurisdiction over Richmondshire and parts of Lancashire. In the event this honour went to the old Benedictine abbey of Chester, and by 1540 glass and lead from the dismantling of Fountains was finding its way into Ripon and York.

The buildings and part of the estates were sold by the king to Sir Richard Gresham in October 1540, and in 1597 the Greshams sold the abbey to Stephen Proctor, son of an early ironmaster. He was later knighted, and built Fountains Hall with stone from the abbey about 1611. After Proctor's death the abbey passed through several hands, coming eventually to the Messenger family who held it until 1768 when it was bought by William Aislabie and incorporated in the ornamental grounds of Studley Royal that had been begun as early as 1716 by his father John Aislabie, Chancellor of the Exchequer. Aislabie landscaped the surroundings of the abbey, cleared parts of the ruins of debris, and built picturesque additions to them that were mostly removed in the following century.

After Aislabie's death in 1781 the estate was held first by his daughter and then by her niece, and during this time the chapter house was excavated by John Martin of Ripon in 1790–91 and repairs were done to the church and the west range in 1822 and 1840. In 1845 the Earl de Grey, descendant of an earlier Aislabie, inherited the property. During his ownership the infirmary and the church were excavated by the Ripon antiquary, John Richard Walbran. Further excavations were carried out by W. H. St J. Hope (later Sir William) in 1887–88 during the ownership of the first Marquis of Ripon.

In 1909 the estate passed to the second Marquis, and on his death in 1923 to Commander G. C. Vyner who continued the tradition of essential repairs to the ruins and cleared parts of the silted bed of the Skell within the abbey. In 1966 the nucleus of the Studley Royal estate was bought by the County Council of the West Riding of Yorkshire, which placed the abbey in the guardianship of what is now the Department of the Environment.

THE ABBOTS OF FOUNTAINS

In common with several other monasteries, Fountains did not give numbers to those abbots who were held to have ruled unwisely. In this list they are given the numbers of their predecessors, followed by a letter.

1	Richard I; prior of York	1132–1139
2	Richard II; sacrist of York, prior of Fountains	1139–1143
3	Henry Murdac; abbot of Vauclair; became archbishop of York 1147, died 1153	1144–1147
3a	Maurice; subprior of Durham, abbot of Rievaulx; resigned	1147–1148
3b	Thorold; monk of Rievaulx; resigned, became abbot of Trois-Fontaines	1148–1150
4	Richard III; precentor of Clairvaux, abbot of Vauclair	1150–1170
5	Robert of Pipewell; abbot of Pipewell	1170–1180
6	William of Newminster; canon of Gisborough, abbot of Newminster	1180–1190
7	Ralph Haget; abbot of Kirkstall	1191–1203
8	John of York; cellarer of Fountains, abbot of Louth Park	1203–1211
9	John of Hessle; became bishop of Ely 1220, died 1225	1211–1220
10	John of Kent; cellarer of Fountains	1220–1247
11	Stephen of Eston; cellarer of Fountains, abbot of Salley, abbot of Newminster	1247–1252
12	William of Allerton; prior of Fountains	1253–1258
13	Adam	1258–1259
14	Alexander	1259–1265
15	Reginald	1265–1274
15a	Peter Alyng; resigned 1279, died 1282	1274–1279
16	Nicholas	1279
17	Adam Ravensworth	1280–1284

17a	Henry Otley; probably resigned 1289, died 1290	1284–1289
17b	Robert Thornton; probably resigned 1290, died 1306	1289–1290
18	Robert Bishopton	1290–1311
19	William Rigton	1311–1316
20	Walter Coxwold; resigned 1336, died 1338	1316–1336
21	Robert Copgrove	1336–1346
22	Robert Monkton	1346–1369
23	William Gower; resigned 1384, died 1390	1369–1384
24	Robert Burley	1384–1410
24a	Roger Frank; monk of Fountains, deposed 1413	1410–1413
25	John Ripon; cellarer of Fountains, abbot of Meaux	1414–1435
26	Thomas Paslew; resigned 1442, died 1443	1435–1442
27	John Martin	1442
28	John Greenwell; monk of Fountains, abbot of Waverley, commissary of the abbot of Cîteaux	1442–1471
29	Thomas Swinton; prior of Fountains; resigned	1471–1478
30	John Darnton; cellarer of Fountains, commissary of the abbot of Cîteaux	1479–1495
31	Marmaduke Huby; monk, bursar and cellarer of Fountains, master of St. Mary Magdalene's Hospital, commissary of the abbot of Cîteaux	1495–1526
32	William Thirsk; commissary of the abbot of Cîteaux; resigned 1536, executed 1537	1526–1536
33	Marmaduke Bradley; monk of Fountains, prebendary of Thorpe, master of St. Mary Magdalene's Hospital; surrendered 1539, died 1553	1536–1539

Building history

Temporary buildings, 1132–c.1138

The Cistercian Order required the founder of a new monastery to provide temporary buildings for the monks before they arrived on the site. When the first monks of Fountains reached Skelldale, however, they belonged to no Order and had no powerful lay benefactor, so they had to make shift as best they could. During the bitter winter of 1132 they first sheltered under the rocks at the side of the dale, and then built a hut beneath a great elm tree near the eastern end of the present precinct, adding a wattle chapel a little later. When Geoffrey d'Ainai was sent from Clairvaux in 1133 to instruct them in the Cistercian way of life they started to erect timber buildings under his guidance, and a mention of carpenters in 1134 suggests that by then these buildings were being supplemented or replaced by more professional structures.

The first stone monastery, c.1138–c.1150

Although a fabric fund was started in 1135, lack of proper endowments probably saw to it that permanent building in stone was not undertaken until the late 1130s. It continued until interrupted by the fire of 1147, and was resumed soon afterwards, by which time the plan of the first monastery had been laid down and most of its buildings had been erected.

The abbey church was from the first designed on a grand scale and had the short, aisleless, square-ended presbytery and square transept chapels characteristic of early Cistercian architecture, although the inner chapels were unusually deep. It was being built during the same years as the second church of Clairvaux and the church of Fontenay and it shared with them not only the main lines of its plan but also many other features that were distinctive of Cistercian building in Burgundy, which are best seen in the transepts. In the nave general Cistercian austerity is shown by the clerestory stated in simplest architectural terms, and by the absence of a triforium stage, whilst influence from the Burgundian cradle of the Order is responsible for the pointed arcades and the pointed barrel vaults set at right angles to them in the aisles. But the heavier and richer Anglo-Norman style contributes the massive cylindrical piers, the arch mouldings, and the capitals and corbels with their scallop and leaf ornament.

By 1147 only the eastern arm of the church and the five easternmost bays of the nave and aisles had been built, satisfying the ritual needs of

23

Isometric plan of the first stone monastery built between c.1138 and c.1150

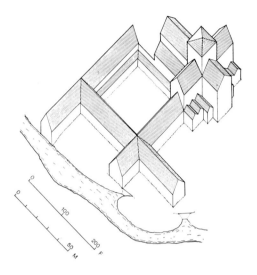

the choir-monks but leaving those of the lay-brothers for the future. The south aisle wall, however, was carried on for nine bays to complete the enclosure of the cloister, which was the same size as it is today.

The claustral buildings that went with this half-finished church were lower and smaller in scale than the present ones, and had none of the characteristics of the plan later adopted by the Order. They followed the old Benedictine arrangement, with day-stairs in the east range and refectory lying parallel to the cloister in the south range.

Enlargement of the monastery, c.1150–1203

When work was resumed about the middle of the century, the nave was completed to its full length of eleven bays without any alteration in design, but increases in the numbers of the brethren forced a decision to remodel the claustral buildings on a much ampler scale. In this rebuilding the features now regarded as characteristic of the Cistercian plan were adopted, with the day-stairs transferred to the south range and the refectory set at right angles to the cloister. Simultaneously, the primitive Cistercian starkness in elevation and detail was abandoned and, as the chronicle puts it, the design of the new buildings was 'far more festive', including rich mouldings and simple forms of carved foliage.

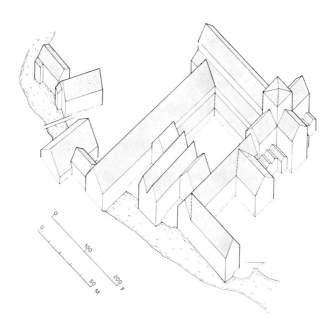

The work went on gradually for half a century, but it can be divided into two main phases. The first probably lasted throughout the time of Abbot Richard III and Abbot Pipewell (1150–80) and saw the rebuilding of the sacristy, chapter house and parlour, the remodelling and lengthening of the dormitory and its undercroft, and the building of a new reredorter farther south than the old one. The northern part of the west range was also rebuilt to a much larger scale, and the lay-brothers' reredorter was added far to the south on the river bank with the intention that the range would eventually be extended to link up with it. To the west, the twin guest houses were also erected.

The second phase occupied the time of Abbot Newminster and Abbot Haget (1180–1203). The west range was extended south to the river, the whole of the south range including kitchen, refectory, warming house and day-stairs was rebuilt, and the lay-brothers' infirmary was added west of their reredorter. In this work the dark, fossiliferous limestone known as Nidderdale 'marble' first began to be used on a small scale, giving contrast to the pale freestone, similar to that provided by Purbeck marble in the south of England.

FA—D   25

Enlargement of the church, 1203–47

The buildings of Fountains had now achieved a scale far exceeding any other monastery of the Order in Britain, but they did not stop growing. By the time of Abbot John of York (1203–11) the old choir and presbytery were too dark and cramped for the number of choir-monks, and their restricted plan was no longer fashionable even with the Cistercians. New plans were therefore made to provide the church with a great aisled eastern arm. Although work had only just started when Abbot John of York died, it is likely that the spectacular eastern transept called the Chapel of the Nine Altars was already envisaged, but the completion of this fell to his successors Abbot John of Hessle and Abbot John of Kent (1211–47).

Abbot John of Kent was an insatiable builder, and he was responsible for many other additions and improvements to the abbey. Under him the new eastern arm of the church was provided with the mosaic tile pavements so much favoured by the northern Cistercians at the time, the cloister alleys were rebuilt, the west guest house was extended, and the lay hospital and almonry in the outer court were enlarged. His main work was the building of the monks' infirmary, carried over the river on a series of tunnels 90yd long and linked to the church by a gallery.

Minor alterations, 1247–1450

After the middle of the thirteenth century little remained to be done. The infirmary chapel was built, the infirmary gallery was extended westwards to meet the claustral buildings, and a building near the infirmary was converted into an apartment for the use of abbots in retirement, probably on the occasion of the resignation of Abbot Alyng in 1279.

The fourteenth century saw no major additions to the abbey, but many minor alterations devoted to improving living conditions within the existing buildings. During this century the lay-brothers ceased to be a significant force in the life of the abbey, a meat diet was sanctioned, and a general demand for better and more modern standards of living led to the creation of private rooms for obedientiaries and senior monks, and of private wards for the sick and aged. The screen walls forming the lay-brothers' choir in the structural nave of the church

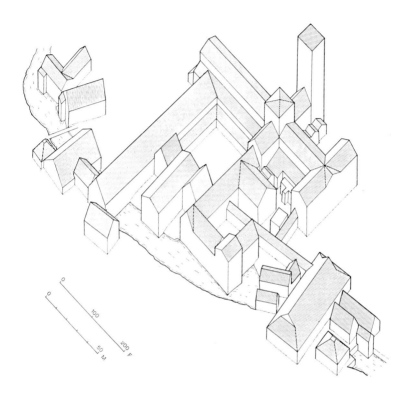

were removed, and the other changes are reflected in the rebuilding of
the infirmary kitchen (where meat was cooked) and by the partitioning
of the aisles of the infirmary hall into individual rooms. The abbot's
house was also extended and improved, probably by Abbot Coxwold
(1316–36), and the internal arrangements of the guest houses were
brought up to date.

The last works, 1450–1526

The middle of the fifteenth century ushered in the last period of
building activity. Abbot Greenwell (1442–71) improved the decoration
and ornaments of the church. Abbot Darnton (1479–95), besides putting
right structural defects in the eastern arm of the church and replacing
the stone vaulting there by timber roofs, inserted the great traceried

windows in the east and west gables. He also extended the practice of making individual chambers in the aisles of the infirmary hall, and did work to the misericord.

This practice was continued by his successor, the great builder Abbot Huby (1495–1526), in whose work magnesian limestone was first extensively used. Abbot Huby left his mark on almost every part of the abbey, but his main works were the remodelling of the abbot's house and the galleries adjacent to it, the addition of the 'church chamber' and a new sacristy on the south side of the presbytery, and the reinforcement of the crossing and transepts, made necessary by structural failure provoked by an earlier attempt to build a tower over the crossing. This also led to his greatest contribution, the building of a new tower on a safe site off the end of the north transept, where it still stands to a height of 160ft as a memorial to the power of Fountains and to the dignity of her abbot.

Description

Visitors coming to Fountains from the Aldfield road and the western car park reach the abbey by what was once its main entrance. They cross the outer court, where Fountains Hall now stands, and enter the great court, represented since Aislabie's day by an expanse of lawn. Here they face the west front of the abbey church with, on its right, the vast length of the west range of claustral buildings presenting its impressively formal and orderly façade to the outer world.

This was not a view that could be enjoyed by the medieval visitor, for the west range which contributes so much to the impression of orderliness and power was then partly masked by the high walls of the cellarer's yards in front of it.

This description begins with the main buildings of the abbey, and deals later with the courts and yards of the precinct and the few buildings that remain in them.

ABBEY CHURCH

The Galilee porch

The ruins of a porch cover the lower part of the west front of the church. Its west wall had a central doorway flanked by open arcades on twin columns, three bays of which were re-erected from fallen fragments in the nineteenth century. These porches were a familiar feature of early Cistercian churches, and were popular places of burial. There are two grave covers at the north end of the porch, and a group of four at the south end, all temporarily covered for protection.

Originally there were two entrances from the porch into the church; an elaborately moulded central doorway, and a plain doorway in the north aisle, later blocked.

The nave

Above the central doorway, the west front is filled by the great Perpendicular window, once of seven lights, inserted by Abbot Darnton in the year before his death, and above this again is a niche holding a headless statue of the Virgin and Child, standing on a corbel carved with the abbot's rebus.*

Inside the church, the lower part of the west front had three large

---

*The crozier of an *abbot* held by the eagle of St *John* the Evangelist, in front of a scroll bearing the date 1494 and the letters *dern*, and standing on a barrel or *tun*.

recesses, the central one occupied by the doorway and the side ones formerly having benches. Above them the arrangement of the twelfth-century windows can still be recognized near the edges of Abbot Darnton's great window. There were three round-headed windows with a circular one above, all enclosed in a round-headed recess the full width of the nave. A doorway in the west wall of the south aisle gives access to spiral stairs that lead up to a passage in the thickness of the aisle wall and so to a gallery across the nave at the level of the sill of this upper recess. From here another set of stairs leads up to the eaves of the nave roof. The main span of the nave always had a wooden roof, the pitch of which was lowered in Abbot Darnton's time, but the aisles had pointed barrel vaults set transversely over each bay, a Burgundian characteristic.

The nave was never meant to be seen or used as a whole. It was from the first divided up by screens, although the ritual arrangements served by them changed during the Middle Ages. Up to the fourteenth century, the seven western bays of the nave formed the choir of the lay-brethren and were shut off from the aisles in every bay except the westernmost by solid stone walls almost 2ft thick. These were not bonded into the piers, but were taken into account from the first, for the mouldings of the pier bases are discontinued where the walls once covered them. The choir stalls of the lay-brethren backed against these walls, and their altar was against the rood screen which crossed the church between the seventh pair of piers from the west, where the holes to support its beam can be seen.

The aisles at this time served only as passages. In the south aisle the west bay has an inserted doorway, later blocked, that led to a pentise outside the cellarium; the second bay has a doorway into the cellarium itself; and the third bay has a doorway to the night-stairs leading up to the dormitory of the lay-brothers over the cellarium. The position of this last doorway was altered slightly when the cellarium was widened later in the twelfth century, and the jamb of its predecessor can be seen just to the east. In the north aisle there is a broad doorway in the sixth bay that perhaps served for bringing materials into the church whilst it was being built, and that was blocked soon afterwards.

After the fourteenth century this part of the church was no longer needed for the lay-brethren. The rood screen and its altar were retained, but the lay-brothers' stalls and the screens behind them were removed throwing the arcades open. The western bays of the nave were now

only used regularly for processions, and the nineteenth-century excavators found beneath the turf a row of 23 limestone slabs of Abbot Huby's time on each side of the nave between the first and fifth piers, with three more in the sixth bay. Each slab had a circle incised on it, and their purpose was to mark the places where the convent made its station before the nave altar towards the end of the Sunday procession.

When the aisles ceased to be used as passages, individual bays were screened off to form chapels. Holes and cuts in the masonry show that five bays of the south aisle and three bays of the north aisle were used in this way. There are also the bases of altars against two piers on the north and two on the south, brackets for statutes on the fourth pier on the north and the fifth on the south, and holes for the reredos of an altar on the west face of the sixth pier on the south. Larger traceried windows were inserted in some of the aisle bays to give more light to these chapels.

The retro-choir

Beyond the rood screen the eighth bay of the nave served as the retro-choir where aged and infirm monks were allowed to sit during the offices. The ninth bay was occupied by chapels of St Mary and St Bernard on each side of the central doorway of the pulpitum, a screen which filled the whole of the tenth bay.

The easternmost bay of the south aisle has a doorway from the church into the cloister. There was a screen shutting this bay off from the transept, and inside the doorway stands the base of a holy water stoup for the use of monks entering the church from the cloister. The marble basin of the stoup is preserved in the abbey museum.

The choir

The choir of the monks filled the eastern bay of the nave and the crossing. It was reached from the retro-choir through the doorway of the pulpitum, which formed its 'lower entrance', and its stalls backed against stone screens which separated it from the aisles and the transepts, and which, like all the screens in the church, have now gone. The nineteenth-century excavations revealed a masonry-lined pit of Abbot Huby's time on each side of the choir, returned against the back of the pulpitum, with recesses in the masonry that had held pottery jars. These pits and their acoustic jars, one of which is preserved in

the abbey museum, formed a hollow space beneath the wooden platforms on which the stalls stood, to give more resonance to the singing. They are at present temporarily covered for preservation.

Farther east there is a large grave cover in the centre of the choir with the indent of a late fifteenth-century brass. It represents an abbot under an elaborate canopy. He holds a crozier, but his mitre is shown just above his head instead of upon it, which may signify that he resigned before death. In that case he would most likely be Abbot Thomas Swinton who resigned in 1478.

Clear of the stalls and just beyond the eastern piers of the crossing there were doorways through the screen walls on either side, forming the 'upper entrance' to the choir. The threshold of the northern door-way remains, and close to it one step of a spiral staircase against the north-east crossing pier, showing that the screen supported a loft or gallery here.

The crossing shows clear signs of the structural failure that resulted in the collapse of its north-east and south-west piers after the dissolution. Its east arch was originally carried on corbels, but when Abbot John of York rebuilt the eastern arm of the church these corbels were underpinned to give more stability. At this time, in accordance with Cistercian custom, the crossing probably carried no more than a low central tower, high enough only to cover the main roofs of the church. It is likely that in the fifteenth century, when architectural austerity was a thing of the past, an attempt was made to heighten this tower, and that the crossing piers began to fail because they had never been intended to carry such a load. Abbot John's work of underpinning had to be reinforced, and a great stepped buttress was built against the west face of the south-east pier. At the top of it there are three much-weathered figures of grotesque beasts.

The south transept

The three arches on the east side of the transept originally led into three chapels that were separated by solid walls. The northernmost of these chapels, which was longer than the others, was destroyed when the eastern arm of the church was rebuilt early in the thirteenth century, but its arch was kept to serve as an entrance to the south aisle of the new presbytery. This arch was altered in Abbot Huby's time, when the state of the crossing was causing concern. The settlement of the south-east crossing pier can be seen in the masonry to the left of the window above this arch, and from that level down to the head of the arch Huby inserted a great 'stitch' of new masonry to bridge a fracture. He also partly blocked the arch itself and put a smaller and massively moulded arch below it to give access to the aisle, placing a shield at each end of its hoodmould. These shields are now heavily weathered, but the northern one bore his initials with a mitre and crozier, and the southern one bore the three horseshoes that were the arms of Fountains in his day.

The lower part of the pier between this arch and the central one is cut back, perhaps to take a large statue of St Christopher, the sight of whom early in the morning was regarded as a good omen for the day. It would be seen by the monks coming down the night-stairs in this transept for the early offices in the church.

The central chapel still has its twelfth-century barrel vault, but the lower part of its east wall was removed in the fifteenth century, leaving the upper part and a segment of a round window supported on an arch, and the chapel was extended eastwards. The new east wall has a Perpendicular window, and a delicately moulded doorway was inserted in the north wall leading to the presbytery aisle. After these alterations the chapel probably served as a sacristy, and a narrow doorway in its south-east corner led to another sacristy of which only the lower stones remain, built by Abbot Huby outside the south aisle of the presbytery. This central chapel now contains the fine early fourteenth-century effigy of a knight, perhaps of the Percy or Mowbray families, a product of the York workshops. It does not belong here, having been moved at least four times since the beginning of the nineteenth century.

The southern chapel remains exactly as it was in the early twelfth century. It has a pointed barrel vault and, in the east wall, a pair of round-headed windows with a circular window above. In the south wall there is a recess that formed a combined piscina and credence, and in the north wall a recess for a cupboard. The step of the altar platform also remains. Just in front of the chapel the nineteenth-century excavators found fragments of the grave cover of a late fifteenth-century monk called John Ripon.

There are two doorways in the south wall of the transept. The eastern one led down to the sacristy in the claustral buildings. The western one is set high and led from the monks' dormitory to the night stairs that once came down into the church against the west wall of the transept, but have now gone. This western doorway belongs to alterations made after the middle of the twelfth century when the east range of claustral buildings outside the transept was remodelled to a more ample scale, and the floor level of the dormitory was set higher than before. The remains of the earlier twelfth-century dormitory doorway can be seen below it on the left, with a half-arch reserved in its blocking to give access to spiral stairs that go up the central buttress of the transept to the top of the gable. Part of the way up these stairs a passage in the thickness of the wall leads eastwards to a room that once existed over the vaults of the transept chapels. Similar rooms existed at other Cistercian abbeys, and may have been used as treasuries.

Like the nave, the transepts had wooden roofs which were lowered in pitch in the fifteenth century, when the two round windows at the top of the south transept gable were blocked.

The north transept

This was originally similar to the south transept, but the alterations made here by Abbot Huby were more extensive, for he blocked the arches of both the central and northern chapels to strengthen the wall near his new tower. There is a doorway in the blocking wall of the central chapel arch, with a bracket for a statue above it and an inscription recording that here was the altar of St Michael the Archangel. The chapel itself has remains of the altar and its platform, a piscina in the south wall, and fragments of a thirteenth-century mosaic tile pavement.

The blocking wall of the north chapel arch also has an inscription, now indecipherable, and an altar set against the wall in the transept. After the arch was blocked, the northern chapel was reached through the central chapel by a doorway forced through the back of its piscina.

The sacrist's office

In the fourteenth century a small building was added to the north side of the northernmost chapel of the transept. It was partly demolished when the tower was built, but its remains show that it had been vaulted and that it had a doorway in its east wall. Its purpose is not certain, but it may have been the sacrist's office, or perhaps a library.

The tower

In the late fifteenth and early sixteenth centuries several northern monasteries added great towers to their churches. At Kirkstall Abbey it was found possible to increase the height of the central tower, but at Shap and Furness attempts to do this ended disastrously, and in each case a tower was built at the west end of the church. Fountains also failed to heighten its central tower, and Abbot Huby decided to build a new one in a safe but unusual position off the north end of the north transept.

It is a tower designed to leave no doubt in the mind about the pre-eminence of Fountains amongst the English Cistercians. Rising to a height of some 160ft, it was divided by floors internally and string courses externally into five storeys. It has a deep moulded plinth, and massive angle buttresses with gablets and niches. The design of the windows varies with each storey, the ground and third floor windows having two-centred heads, the first floor four-centred or elliptical heads, and the top floor flat heads. Bands of inscription are placed beneath the embattled parapet and beneath the two upper tiers of windows. The Latin texts are taken from the Cistercian breviary and include the verse from the first epistle to Timothy: *Regi autem saeculorum immortali, invisibili, soli Deo, honor et gloria in saecula saeculorum* (Now unto the King eternal, immortal, invisible, the only God, be honour and glory for ever and ever), repeated four times in abbreviated forms and much used by Abbot Huby on his other buildings.

The top of the tower was designed to have two large pinnacles at each angle, standing out on the face of the buttresses and connected to the parapet by miniature flying buttresses, with a smaller pinnacle set diagonally and corbelled out from the parapet in the middle of each side.

In addition to the inscriptions, the external faces of the tower have niches set above seven of the windows, some still containing their statues. On the south face, a niche over the lowest window has a statue of an abbot without a mitre, perhaps representing St Benedict or St Bernard. On the north face a niche over the lowest window has St Catherine with her martyr's palm, and over the window above is St James the Great. The niches over the lowest windows on the east and west faces are surmounted by angels holding shields of arms, that on the east bearing the three horseshoes of Fountains Abbey, and that on the west the mitre, crozier and initials of Abbot Huby.

Shields of arms are also inserted in the bands of inscription. The horseshoes of Fountains appear six times, the maunch or sleeve of Norton of Norton Conyers appears four times, an unidentified shield bearing a cross between two mitres and two keys appears twice.

The presbytery

The twelfth-century presbytery was aisleless, square-ended, and only two bays long, following Cistercian practice in all these things. The line of its foundations and those of the inner transept chapels, all destroyed during the thirteenth-century rebuilding, are indicated by markers set in the turf.

The thirteenth-century presbytery, started by Abbot John of York, continued by Abbot John of Hessle, and completed by Abbot John of Kent, all between 1203 and 1247, is five bays long and has north and south aisles that absorb the sites of the old inner chapels of the transepts. The main arcades and the walls they supported have gone entirely; in all probability they were severely damaged when the crossing arches collapsed after the dissolution, and their debris was removed when Aislabie tidied up this part of the church in the eighteenth century. The eastern responds of the arcade and the surviving south-west respond, together with fragments found on the site, show that the piers were alternately octagonal and clustered, the latter having a diamond-shaped freestone core with substantial attached shafts at the angles and four more slender detached shafts to the diagonals.

The aisle walls stand almost to their full height, their lancet windows in each bay flanked by curious ramping arches designed to fit beneath the curve of the vaults. There are slight differences in the external design of the aisles. On the north side the external buttresses ended in steep-pitched gablets and there was a gable over the window in each bay. On the south the buttresses had pinnacles and the walls had a horizontal parapet and corbel table. On both sides there were once flying buttresses crossing the aisles to support the stone vault of the main span of the presbytery.

Little is left of the ritual arrangements of the presbytery. Like the choir, it was enclosed by stone screen walls along the line of the piers, returned across its east end as an open arcade on triple shafts supporting a gallery. In the west bay, between the first pair of piers, are the two presbytery steps with stone treads rebated to take a tiled floor; they are at present temporarily covered for protection. On the north side of the third bay there is a stone coffin, probably of an important benefactor. In the easternmost bay a tiled platform of two steps represents the site of the high altar. In its present position and form it is probably eighteenth-century work of Aislabie's time, but it is made up of thirteenth-century mosaic tiles from the pavement that Abbot John of Kent laid in this part of the church.

The Chapel of the Nine Altars

Beyond the presbytery the thirteenth-century work develops into a great eastern transept, completed in the time of Abbot John of Kent, and known in the Middle Ages as the Chapel of the Nine Altars from the number of individual chapels it contained. The only parallel to this

Plan of the abbey precincts

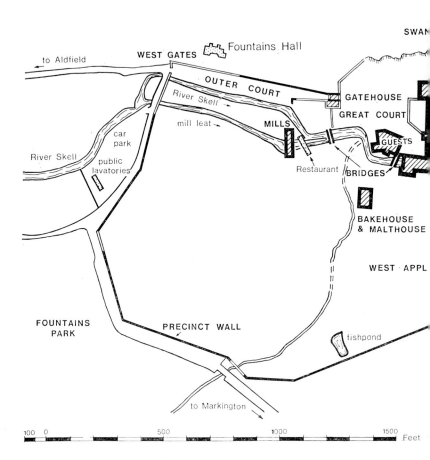

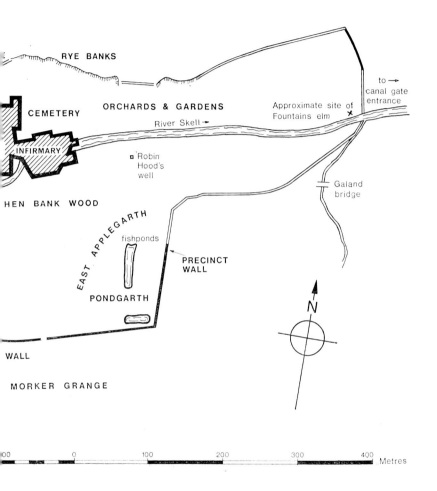

RYE BANKS

ORCHARDS & GARDENS

River Skell →

Approximate site of
Fountains elm

to →
canal gate
entrance

CEMETERY

INFIRMARY

□ Robin
Hood's
well

HEN BANK WOOD

EAST APPLEGARTH

fishponds

Galand
bridge

PRECINCT
WALL

PONDGARTH

N

WALL

MORKER GRANGE

| 00 | 0 | 100 | 200 | 300 | 400 |
Metres

remarkable feature is the similar chapel at Durham Cathedral, begun in 1242 in emulation of the work at Fountains.

The chapel extends eastwards for the equivalent of two bays of the presbytery, and projects in three narrower bays to the north and south, giving it a total width equivalent to that of the main transepts and crossing. The lines of the presbytery arcades are carried across it to the east wall by twin arches supported on slender octagonal piers almost 50ft high, once surrounded by eight detached marble shafts bound to the pier by a moulded ring. There are two tiers of windows, the upper ones with their wall-passage probably reflecting the design of the vanished clerestory of the presbytery. The gables originally had groups of lancets, perhaps with a wheel window above, and the bases of two small buttresses on the outside plinth show that the central gable at the east end had a group of three lancets. There is a doorway with a finely moulded round head in the north wall, leading to the cemetery, and a similar doorway in the south wall leading to the infirmary passage. Smaller doorways in the angles gave access to spiral stairs leading up to the wall-passage and the roofs.

Many of the ritual arrangements survive in this part of the church. A low platform runs in front of the east wall, and the nine altars stood on this. There were three in the northern projection of the chapel, three more closely spaced in the large central bay, and three in the southern projection. The bases of several of the altars remain, and fragments of the stone paving of the platform. Set in the pavement on the right-hand side of each altar there was once a shallow drain or floor-piscina, and a few of these have survived. Each altar also had its aumbries or cupboards set in the wall behind it. In the thirteenth century the nine chapels were separated from one another by solid stone screen walls just over 8ft high, with a gabled coping.

These original arrangements underwent several alterations, mostly in the latter part of the fifteenth century. The stone screens were taken down and replaced by wooden ones, and the three altars of the central bay were replaced by a single larger one, the base of which remains. Several of the cupboards were also blocked up. At this time, the northernmost altar was dedicated to St James the Apostle and an inscription recording this, scratched on the plastered surface of the north wall, survived until the present century but has now weathered away.

As first built, the Chapel of the Nine Altars was vaulted in stone throughout, but its sheer eastern wall did not provide sufficient abutment, and by the late fifteenth century it betrayed signs of being forced outwards. In 1483 Abbot Darnton set about the repair and modernization of the chapel. He took down the vaults, cutting their springers back to the wall face, and replaced them by wooden roofs, adjusting the gables to suit their lower pitch. In the course of this work he rebuilt the twin arches carried by the octagonal piers in the centre of the chapel, and to give more abutment to the east wall he increased the projection of the two buttresses outside the central bay and stitched up the fractures that had developed in the stonework. A gap in the head of the north window of the east wall was filled with stonework carved with a head, a rose, and an angel bearing a scroll with the date 1483, and a similar gap in the head of the east window of the south wall has stonework bearing his rebus, an abbot's head, a scroll between two fish, a figure of St James, and an abbreviated form of the abbey's motto: *Benedicite Fontes Domino*. He also replaced the windows in both storeys of the central bay by a vast traceried window once of nine lights, and either he or his successor, Abbot Huby, replaced the upper windows in both end gables by traceried windows of seven lights.

Abbot Huby was also probably responsible for replacing the window above the south doorway of the chapel by a large round-headed arch. This gave access from the upper storey of the infirmary gallery to a wooden pew cantilevered out into the south end of the chapel allowing the abbot, with whose house that gallery communicated, to participate in the offices without coming down into the church.

THE CLOISTER AND ITS BUILDINGS

The main buildings of the abbey lie to the south of the church and form ranges enclosing three sides of the rectangular court known as the cloister, the nave of the church forming the fourth side.

The east range has on the ground floor a passage, the chapter house, the parlour, and then a long room projecting south beyond the cloister. The whole of the first floor was occupied by the dormitory of the monks.

The south range has the refectory of the monks in the centre, with

43

the warming house and day-stairs to the dormitory on its east side, and the kitchen on its west side.

The west range has the cellarium or storehouse of the abbey on the ground floor, prolonged far to the south as the refectory of the lay-brethren. The whole of the first floor is their dormitory.

The cloister

The cloister is about 125ft square, and once had a covered alley on each side, the lean-to roof of which has left marks on the surrounding buildings. Fragments of the alley walls survived until 1770, but there are no visible remains today, although the foundations were traced in the nineteenth-century excavations. These alleys were rebuilt by Abbot John of Kent, and fragments found in the excavations show that the walls had open arcades standing on twin shafts with marble capitals carved with conventional foliage.

Near the centre of the cloister garth there is a massive octagonal stone basin on a rough platform. It was brought here from the cellarium in 1859, where it had been in use as a cider press. Its original position and purpose are not known.

The north alley of the cloister was used by the monks for reading and study, although there are now no remains of the benches on which they sat against the church wall. Immediately west of the doorway from the church there was a large recess in the wall with a smaller one on each side of it, all later blocked with masonry. The arm of the south transept that overlaps the cloister has in its wall a large round-headed recess that served as the cupboard for the books used in the cloister. On the face of the buttress just south of it a shallow rectangular recess has been cut into the masonry; this is a very rare feature indeed, for it was intended to hold the wooden frame containing the *tabula* or wax tablet on which were written the names of the monks with special duties for the week.

The passage

Alongside the south transept the east range of claustral buildings is pierced by a ground-floor passage leading from the cloister to the yard and sacristy south of the presbytery. This passage now extends the full width of the transept, but in the early twelfth century it was shorter, being closed by a wall just east of the doorway into the transept. At this time it was also subdivided by a partition into an eastern part used as a sacristy, with a doorway into the transept, and a western part used as a library, with a doorway into the cloister. Later in the twelfth century the partition and the east wall were taken down, and a new east wall with a doorway was built as a continuation southwards of the wall of the transept chapels. The five eastern bays of the passage were then provided with a ribbed vault, but the western bay has a half-barrel vault supporting the night-stairs to the dormitory above.

After the dissolution, the passage was filled with human bones, estimated to represent at least 400 skeletons and probably coming from graves ransacked in the church and the cemetery. Its east and west doorways were then walled up. They were reopened in 1854, when the bones were taken away and reburied.

The chapter house

This is the next room to the south, with a magnificent group of three elaborately moulded arches to the cloister. It was the administrative and disciplinary centre of the abbey, where the convent met each day under the presidency of the abbot to commemorate the saints and their dead brethren, to hear a chapter of the Rule of St Benedict, to confess faults and receive punishment, and to transact business as a corporate body. It is one of the largest chapter houses in the country, six bays long and projecting well beyond the main range of buildings. It replaced an earlier and smaller chapter house contained within the walls of the range.

The interior was vaulted in three aisles from two rows of marble columns. The column capitals, one of which is preserved in the museum, were carved with conventional foliage. Around the walls, the vault was carried on corbels carved with a variety of scallop and leaf designs, and it can be seen from the two little shafts standing on the second pair of corbels from the west that the six western compartments of the vault were lower than the rest, to allow the dormitory floor to cross above without changing level.

These western bays served as a vestibule, and the northern and southern compartments of the westernmost bay were once walled off to serve as book cupboards, entered from the cloister by the two flanking arches, with the central arch alone acting as the doorway to the chapter house.

Beyond the vestibule there are stone platforms in three tiers against the side walls and the east wall. These were the footpaces to support the benches on which the monks sat in chapter, the gap in the middle of the east end being for the abbot's chair.

In most monasteries it was customary to bury the abbots in the chapter house, and their graves can be seen here clustered in the two eastern bays. The first five abbots of Fountains died and were buried away from their abbey,* but nineteen out of the next twenty-one were buried in this room,† the last being Abbot Copgrove in 1346, after which date they were buried in the church.

Close to the east wall, in front of the gap in the footpaces, there is a group of five graves. The northernmost has been identified as that of Abbot Adam I (1259). The next to the south has lost its cover slab, but may well be that of Abbot John of York (1211). The large slab in the centre belongs to the great builder, Abbot John of Kent (1247), and to the south of him lies Abbot William of Allerton (1258). The last grave on the south has not been identified, nor has any of the four graves in the second row, between the first pair of columns from the east, but it can be seen that these last are probably the earliest ones, for John of Kent and his neighbours have been crowded into the space at their feet. It is therefore likely that this second row contains the graves of Abbot Richard III (1170), Abbot Robert of Pipewell (1180), Abbot William of Newminster (1190). and Abbot Ralph Haget (1203). At the head of the southernmost grave in the second row there is a square stone slab with a socket for the shaft of the lectern, and Abbot William Rigton (1316) is known to have been buried just to the west of this, although there are no remains of his grave. There are two more unidentified grave covers opposite the second pair of columns from the east, the northern one having the matrix of a fourteenth-century brass, and there are fragments of three more graves midway between the second and third pairs of columns. Another grave lies in the westernmost bay on the north side, and this may have belonged to Abbot Henry Otley (1289) who is known to have been buried near the entrance. The stone coffin against the north wall was probably placed

---

*Richard I at Rome; Richard II at Clairvaux; Henry Murdac at York; Maurice probably at Rievaulx; Thorold at Trois-Fontaines.
†The exceptions are John of Hessle and Stephen of Eston, who were buried at Ely and Vaudey respectively.

there after the chapter house was excavated in 1790–91. The excavations of 1856 also revealed a group of graves, probably belonging to important benefactors, in the east alley of the cloister just in front of the chapter house doorway. These are no longer visible.

The parlour

The fine doorway of the parlour is designed to match the three archways of the chapter house. The parlour was the place where essential conversation between the monks was allowed, silence being generally observed elsewhere in the monastic buildings. It is little more than a passage through the range, with another doorway at its east end. The three bays of vaulting are carried by triple corbels carved with unusual and severely beautiful leaf designs.

The dormitory undercroft

The last doorway on the east side of the cloister leads into a long room once vaulted in seven double bays from a central row of piers, The northernmost bay, which has a doorway in its east wall, formed a through passage from the cloister to the infirmary, and was shut off from the rest of the room by a wall on the line of the first pier. This wall was pulled down about the middle of the nineteenth century, when the ruins were being cleared of debris.

The fourth bay from the north (including the bay once used as a passage) has a doorway in its west wall, leading to two small vaulted chambers contrived in the block that supports the day-stairs. The sixth bay had doorways in both east and west walls, the latter blocked when the buildings in the yard of the warming house were erected. Just beyond these doorways there are signs that a partition once crossed the room, making a separate chamber out of the southernmost bay, with two windows looking on to the river and a passage through the wall to a privy corbelled out over the water. This passage was also later blocked.

This undercroft is a later twelfth-century remodelling of an early twelfth-century building, much of which remains incorporated in its walls. To the north of the doorway from the cloister can be seen the outline of an earlier doorway, blocked up, which once led to the day-stairs that occupied this position in Cistercian monasteries until the middle of the twelfth century. These stairs therefore took up what is now the north bay of the undercroft, and there was a little room beneath them, the window of which survives in the east wall. The passage to the infirmary came next, and its blocked doorways can be seen in both walls just south of the first pier. Opposite the fifth pier there is a straight joint in each wall, and beyond this point the whole of the southern end of the undercroft was completely rebuilt in the later twelfth century. In its earlier form, however, the straight joints were the northern responds of a pair of large arches that pierced the east and west walls of the south end of the room.

The early twelfth-century undercroft was not vaulted, but had a wooden ceiling giving only 7ft headroom.

The use to which the later twelfth-century undercroft was put is not known, but in its earlier twelfth-century form it was probably a workroom associated with the discipline of manual labour favoured by the Cistercians in their early days. The open arches at the south end would then lead to work yards on both sides of the room.

The dormitory

This occupied the whole of the first floor of east range, running south from the transept for 178ft, with a projection 55ft long over the eastern part of the chapter house. Most of its walls have gone except over the chapter house and the north end of the undercroft. It was entered by two stairways, the night-stairs leading up from the south transept, and the day-stairs in the south-east angle of the cloister.

At the north end, the part of the dormitory over the eastern bays of the sacristy passage formed a separate little room, at first with a round-headed archway in its west wall, later reduced in size to a doorway. It was once vaulted, and has a cupboard in its south wall. Like the nearby room over the transept chapels, it was probably a treasury or strong room in the charge of the sacrist, who usually had his bed at this end of the dormitory so that he could be near the abbey clock in the south transept, by which he regulated the times of the offices in church.

The part of the dormitory over the chapter house had its floor at a higher level than the rest, and was lit by round-headed windows spaced some 15ft apart. The rest of the dormitory had similar but larger windows spaced from 18 to 21ft apart, with smaller rectangular windows between.

In a monastic dormitory the beds were usually placed against the side walls, leaving a central space in which, at Clairvaux, stood great wardrobes for the monks' clothes. In some houses it was the practice to place the beds of the novices between those of the monks, for better supervision, and the alternating types of windows here at Fountains may be a sign of this. Later in the Middle Ages, to keep pace with increasing demands for more privacy, dormitories were usually divided into cubicles by wooden partitions, and some of the holes in the walls between the windows here may have been for that purpose. Another late alteration was the insertion of a narrow doorway in the south wall of the projection over the chapter house, from which a bridge led to the upper storey of the infirmary gallery.

The line of the high-pitched roof of the dormitory can be seen on the south transept gable, with two openings that led from the spiral stairs in the transept buttress to lofts contrived in the roof.

In the early twelfth century the dormitory was much lower, and parts of its east wall remain in the undercroft where they were covered by the stone vault that replaced the earlier flat ceiling of that room. Here it can be seen that the earlier dormitory had much smaller round-headed windows, spaced 13ft apart. Two pairs of these windows remain, and between them are a blocked round-headed doorway and a small blocked opening to the north of it. The doorway led to the early twelfth-century reredorter which projected eastwards from the dormitory at this point, and the opening was to house the lamp which was kept burning at night to give some light to both reredorter and dormitory.

The reredorter

The position of the early twelfth-century reredorter or latrine block is shown by the doorway and lamp niche mentioned above. It was 31ft wide, and projected eastwards from the dormitory. Within the building, the drain ran along the south side and was flushed by an underground channel from the river. This reredorter was 96ft long, and some parts of its eastern end are incorporated in the abbot's house. In this part of the building the drain was vaulted, and three privies, accessible only from outside its south wall discharged into it.

When the dormitory was remodelled and heightened later in the twelfth century, the greater part of the old reredorter was demolished and a new one was built along the river bank off the south end of the new dormitory. At first it was intended that a new drain should be built down the centre of the new reredorter, and doorways were provided in the east wall of the dormitory undercroft north and south of the proposed line of this drain. When work started, however, it was decided to put the drain along the south side of the building, and the southern doorway had to be blocked. This new drain is well preserved, and it opened on to the river by a series of four arches the piers of which, pointed like the cutwaters of a bridge, remain together with the massive arch at its eastern end.*

*When the silt was removed from the drain during the nineteenth-century excavations, a hoard of 354 silver coins ranging in date up to the time of Charles I was found beneath this arch. They were probably buried during local disturbances in the Civil War.

North of the drain, the basement of the reredorter formed a long room, once vaulted in five bays, but later divided by a thick cross wall. It has a doorway (later blocked), a fireplace and a window in its north wall. Its purpose is not known with certainty, but at Pontigny a similar room was used by the novices. The sanitary arrangements were on the vanished first floor, reached directly from the dormitory, the latrine seats being ranged along the south wall discharging into the drain beneath.

The day-stairs

This impressive flight of 30 steps is reached through an archway at the east end of the south range of claustral buildings. It was built towards the end of the twelfth century, and replaced an earlier flight in the east range. There are holes for the attachment of a handrail on the right-hand side of the steps and, above these, holes for beams that once supported the floor of a loft over the lower part of the flight. Higher still, it can be seen that the staircase was once vaulted in stone.

The landing at the top of the steps had three doorways, only one of which now survives. A doorway on the left once led to the dormitory; one in front led to the first floor of a building in the warming house yard; the surviving one on the right leads to a room over the warming house.

The warming house

This lies to the west of the day-stairs, with a doorway from the cloister. Its name describes its purpose, for in early days it was the only room in the monastery, except for the kitchens and infirmaries, where a fire was kept burning during the winter months so that the monks could restore circulation to their chilled limbs after hours spent in the cold of the cloister and the church. The Cistercians also used it for the periodical bleeding of the brethren for reasons of health.

The room has a fine ribbed vault springing from a central pier, and the whole of its east wall is taken up by two vast fireplaces. The northern one was later blocked and its chimney was dismantled, but the southern one remains intact, supported by a modern wooden frame, and it has a remarkable flat lintel of joggled stones with a span of 16ft. In the west wall there are two openings into the refectory to provide that room with a little borrowed heat, and the south wall has

The day-stairs at the south-east angle of the cloister

two acutely pointed archways the full height of the vault, leading into the yard beyond. The lower part of the eastern archway is grooved for boards or shutters, later replaced by a rough blocking wall, whilst the lower part of the western archway has a more carefully built wall with a doorway in it.

The warming house yard

The warming house yard extends southwards to the river, shut in on one side by the refectory and on the other by the dormitory undercroft against which there was a narrow building, now much ruined. This building was once vaulted in two bays, and had two large archways to the yard that were later blocked. It probably served as a wood store for the warming house fires. Midway along the south wall of the building are the massive corbels of a privy discharging into the river from a room that once existed on the first floor.

The west side of the yard was covered by a pentise along the refectory wall, and from the south end of this a wooden footbridge, supported on the cutwater at the south-east angle of the refectory, once crossed the river, enabling fuel to be brought into the yard without going through the cloister.

The muniment room

The doorway on the west side of the landing at the top of the day-stairs leads to a short vaulted passage. There was a second door 5ft along the passage fastened by a long cabin-hook or iron stay that has left a circular mark on the wall. Beyond this a doorway leads northward into a well preserved room vaulted in four bays from a central pier like the warming house below. The triplets of lancets in its north wall looked out over the cloister garth, above the roof of the cloister alley. The floor is of medieval tiles found during the clearance of the sacristy passage and set here with others in 1856.

This room was designed with security in mind. Its windows had iron bars, and to break into it the two doors in the passage and the door into the room itself, which had a drawbar, would have to be forced. Being over the warming house it was also one of the driest rooms in the abbey, and the stone vaulting above and below it gave some protection from fire. In all probability it served as a muniment room where the abbey's archives were kept. Its size is not surprising when it is remembered that in addition to the convent's archives (and Fountains had more than 3 500 title-deeds to its extensive lands) it probably housed the deeds and treasure of local secular lords, for the great abbeys often acted as safe-deposits for these. The memory of its former use may explain why the Court of the Liberty of Fountains continued to be held in it for some three centuries after the dissolution.

Between the two doors in the passage there was once a third doorway to spiral stairs that led up to a room over the muniment room. Little remains of this, but it seems to have been used for storage of goods hauled up by tackle into a doorway with a projecting threshold that overhangs the yard.

The south doorway on the day-stairs landing led to another room, now gone, over the wood store in the yard. It was intended for domestic use because it was served by the privy, the corbels of which can be seen in the yard. It probably communicated with the dormitory and may have been a chamber for the prior.

The laver

The doorway in the middle of the south range leads to the refectory or dining hall of the monks, and on each side of it the wall facing the cloister was taken up by the laver or long wash-basin used by the brethren before meals. It has a stone bench that once supported a semi-circular trough that held the water. The inner side of this trough remains but the outer side, which was probably of metal, has gone. Each trough was supplied with running water from a lead pipe near the middle; the holes for these pipes, and the vertical chases for the pipes draining the troughs can still be seen.

The troughs were set in deep wall arcades, the outer orders of which were once carried on shafts standing on the stone benches.

The towel cupboard

Between the warming house doorway and the day-stairs there is a large round-headed cupboard, the jambs of which have been cut back for double doors. This was the towel cupboard used in association with the laver.

The refectory

The refectory is one of the noblest rooms in the abbey, measuring

47 by 110ft and so projecting far to the south of the main range of buildings. Its south end is carried over the river on a vaulted tunnel. Excavations in 1904 showed that this refectory replaced an early twelfth-century one built on an east-west axis, a plan favoured by the older monastic orders and by the Cistercians themselves up to the middle of the twelfth century.

The room is entered from the cloister by an elaborately moulded doorway, and it was originally divided into two aisles by an arcade carried on four columns which have now gone, although the stone plinth of the southernmost survives as well as the corbels from which the arcade sprang. It had an M-roof in two spans, and the south wall therefore had twin gables, each with a pair of lancets and a circular window above. Later in the Middle Ages the pitch of the roof was lowered and the circular windows were blocked. Each side wall is lit by a range of six shafted lancets.

Conduct during meals was strictly regulated, and the refectory shows many of the arrangements necessary for this. Against the south wall and the southern parts of the east and west walls there is a low platform on which the dining tables stood. The south platform is broader and higher than the others, and it formed the dais for the high table where the prior presided over meals, custom requiring the abbot to eat with the guests. In the centre of the wall over the prior's place there are pinholes to support the crucifix that acted as a reredos to the high table.

Each side platform had two long tables carried on stone legs, some of which remain. Between the tables there were narrow passages with stone jambs, giving access to the benches on which the monks sat with their backs to the walls. The western platform is prolonged north-wards to accommodate the sideboard and the lockers for table linen and spoons.

Silence during meals was interrupted only by a reading from the Bible, and the pulpit for this is in the west wall. It is reached by a small doorway which leads to stairs mounting southwards in a passage in the wall in front of the three northern lancets. On the right, just inside the doorway, is a locker for the reader's books. The passage and stairs were once vaulted and their inner wall had an open arcade that matched the windows in the outer wall. At the top of the stairs there is a landing, and a great corbel carved with leaf designs projects from it into the room to carry the pulpit.

The kitchen

The kitchen is placed at the west end of the south range where it could serve the refectory of the monks on the east and the refectory of the lay-brothers on the west. It has a doorway to the cloister and a service-hatch that looks like a doorway into the refectory. The inner order of this hatch does not extend to the full height of the jambs and is slightly concave, for it was designed to take a dresser door revolving on a pivot. Dishes could be placed on the shelves of this revolving dresser in the kitchen, and it could then be turned for unloading in the refectory.

Most of the kitchen's internal structures have gone, but their arrangement can be made out. The room was divided into two parts by two great fireplaces standing back to back in the centre of the floor and carrying a common flue that went up through the middle of the roof. The spaces between the sides of the fireplaces and the east and west walls of the room were vaulted as passages. The eastern passage remains complete, and the springers for the vault of the western one can be seen on the wall. The main vault of the kitchen was a complicated one. Above the passages there were barrel vaults abutting the central flue on both sides. North of the fireplaces there was a ribbed vault in three bays, and south of them a vault in two bays was later inserted.

The north wall of the kitchen has three small cupboards. The south wall has a single cupboard, and a doorway and large archway to the yard outside. This part of the kitchen has beamholes for a loft at the level of the passage vaults, perhaps used for storage.

There was a room over the kitchen, but it is almost completely gone. It could be reached from the dormitory of the lay-brothers, and was probably a chamber for their master.

The kitchen yard

The kitchen yard lies between the refectory and the west range. It is separated from the river by a wall with the remains of a privy near its east end. A pentise ran along the south wall of the kitchen and returned down the west wall of the refectory, giving covered access to this privy and to a wooden footbridge across the river, similar to that in the warming house yard. Goods and fuel could be brought from the south bank of the river into the yard by this bridge, and so into the kitchen by the large archway in its south wall.

The west range

The west range of the claustral buildings is the largest of its kind in Europe, 300ft long and vaulted in 22 double bays from a central line of piers from which the ribs spring without capitals. It was used for the bulk stores of the convent, and for the accommodation of the lay-brethren who, in this position, were in direct contact with their work in the great court.

The early twelfth-century west range was much smaller than the present one, being only some 25ft wide but extending as far south as the river. When the northern part of the range was remodelled later in the twelfth century in the form in which we now see it, the old east wall was retained but a new west wall was built farther out to give the building a width of 42ft. The doorways and windows in these northern thirteen bays have round heads, and the buttresses are half-octagons. At the end of the twelfth century the range was extended southwards by another nine bays, its southern end being carried right across the river on four vaulted tunnels. In this part of the building the windows have pointed heads and the buttresses are rectangular. The whole range was vaulted at this later date, and buttresses were added on the cloister side of the early east wall to abut this new vault.

Despite these differences of detail, the range has a general uniformity of style that belies its complex building history. The great uninterrupted expanse of the ground floor, today providing one of the most famous views in the abbey, is also deceptive in its unity, for it originally served a number of different purposes and was divided by several cross-walls that were not demolished until the abbey fell into ruin.

One of these cross-walls shut off the two northern bays from the rest, forming a room of which the central part is taken up by a great block of masonry pierced by two arches that support the lay-brethren's night-stairs above. In the early twelfth century this room was an outer parlour giving access from the great court to the cloister, and it had a doorway of this date in the middle of its east wall. Later in the century, when the range has widened and the night-stairs were put in, this doorway was blocked because it fell inconveniently behind the central pier of the stair block, but the room retained its old function and was provided with a new east doorway in the south bay. Very late in the Middle Ages it ceased to be used as a parlour, and this second doorway was blocked.

57

The cellarium

The cellarium or storehouse of the abbey occupied the next six bays, and a substantial wall once crossed the eighth bay to cut it off from the rest of the range. There was another wall across the sixth bay, dividing the storage space into two rooms of four and two bays respectively. The sixth bay has a large arch in the west wall, for bringing heavy goods into the building.

The outer parlour

The ninth and tenth bays were also walled off to form a second or cellarer's parlour and entry to the cloister. The ninth bay has an arch in the west wall and a doorway in the east wall, and alongside the latter is a narrow loop, later blocked, through which those in charge of the entry could see what was happening in the cloister before admitting anyone to it.

The lay-brothers' refectory

The southern twelve bays of the range were the refectory of the lay-brothers, entered in the eleventh bay of the west wall by an archway opposite the foot of their day-stairs. In the east wall of the same bay there was a service hatch from the kitchen, blocked after the lay-brothers had ceased to be a significant force in the life of the abbey, and in the twelfth bay of the west wall what now appears to be a round-headed doorway was a cupboard recess. These two bays formed a service or 'screens' end, and the refectory proper occupied the southern ten bays, making it appreciably longer although not as wide as the refectory of the monks.

The cellarer's office

Midway along the range a small building is attached to the outside of its west wall opposite the twelfth and thirteenth bays. It is approached from the north by a passage with a recess for a cupboard on its west side. The room itself is complete and unaltered, with its three windows, its hooded fireplace, and an irregular ribbed vault designed to allow the lay-brothers' day-stairs to pass over it. This was the cellarer's office, ideally placed for checking the stores as they were brought into the cellarium, and it is the only example that has survived intact from so early a date.

A pentise ran north from this office outside the west wall of the range, and was returned along the side of the church for a short way, where it covered a doorway into the south aisle of the nave. This was the way by which the lay-brothers went under cover from their day-stairs to the church, and the doorway was blocked later in the Middle Ages when they no longer used the nave.

The cellarer's yards

Two yards enclosed by high walls lay outside the west wall of the range north of the cellarer's office. The dividing wall between the yards was opposite the fifth bay of the range, but nothing remains of them now. They served to isolate transport unloading before the cellarium doors from the rest of the traffic in the great court.

The lay-brothers' day-stairs

The lay-brothers' day-stairs rise to the south as an open flight of steps opposite the eleventh bay, and lead to a landing over the vault of the cellarer's office. This landing was roofed, and from it another flight of steps rises eastwards to the lay-brothers' dormitory.

The lay-brothers' dormitory

The lay-brothers' dormitory occupies the whole of the first floor of the west range. It is the largest of its kind in existence, its floor area of 12 600 sq ft indicating the need to accommodate great numbers of lay-brethren in the twelfth century. It lacks only its roof and parts of its east wall opposite the kitchen. The present floor is modern, designed to waterproof the vault below.

Like the ground floor of the west range, the southern nine bays of the dormitory are later in date than the rest. But whereas the windows in the later part of the ground floor are pointed, the dormitory windows are round-headed throughout, for the builders of the southern part had it in mind that their work would be seen internally as a single space with the northern half, and they sacrificed modernity of detail to uniformity of effect.

The dormitory is not accessible to visitors.

The lay-brothers' reredorter

The lay-brothers' reredorter projects westwards from the south end of their dormitory. It was built at about the same time as the northern half of the west range to which it was linked when the range was later extended southwards.

The reredorter is built over the river, and its lower storey is divided by a spine wall. Its south wall has a row of nine arches to take latrines that were reached from the south bank of the river, outside the building, and were later enclosed by a pentise connected to the lay-brothers' infirmary. The first floor, reached from the dormitory, probably had a wooden partition on top of the spine wall, with the latrine seats placed back to back against it in two rows over the two channels into which the river below is divided.

THE ABBOT'S HOUSE

Early Cistercian custom required the abbot to sleep in the dormitory, but as time went on the duties of his office made it more and more desirable for him to have lodgings of his own. One of the first expedients was to build a lodging for him near the end of the reredorter, through which he could remain technically in touch with the dormitory.

It is not known where the early abbots of Fountains had their rooms, but by the fourteenth century they were established in a building near the east end of the monks' reredorter. When the new reredorter had been built about the middle of the twelfth century, its predecessor to the north was demolished except for its eastern end, and in the fourteenth century the abbot's house occupied this block and stretched southwards to meet the later reredorter.

Only the basement of this building remains, and it has a complex history. The dates of the various alterations are best understood by referring to the plan. In the time of Abbot Coxwold, about 1320, the house extended from the north wall of the old reredorter to the north wall of the new one, and its basement was divided by a wall into a narrow western and a wider eastern part. The eastern part was subdivided into two rooms by the south wall of the old reredorter in which a group of three latrine shafts can be seen, blocked up in the fourteenth century but now exposed again by the collapse of the blocking. Access to the northern room was by a doorway in its north wall and by spiral stairs leading down from the rooms above. The southern room has the base of a bay window built outside its east wall.

The narrower western part was subdivided into three little cells which were prisons for recalcitrant monks. Each had an iron staple for the prisoner's chains (the northernmost remains fixed in the stone pavement) and two had latrines, one of which could be flushed by pouring a bucket of water through a channel contrived in its west wall. In the nineteenth century the remains of an inscription scratched on the wall of the southernmost cell could still be deciphered as *vale libertas* (farewell liberty). There can be little doubt that the monk William Esteby was a prisoner in one of these cells when he was freed from his shackles and rescued during an armed assault on the abbey in 1423.

In Abbot Huby's time (1495–1526) the house was extended southwards to absorb the eastern end of the later reredorter. The two eastern bays of the reredorter were cut off from the rest by a thick partition wall with spiral stairs to the rooms above, the base for another great bay window was built against the east wall, and the easternmost arch of the great drain was blocked by the base for a third bay window on the south. Stairs were also built leading up from the infirmary passage to the first floor at the north end of the house.

The arrangements of the house have to be inferred from the plan of the basements only. As remodelled by Abbot Huby, its main entrance was from the infirmary passage, where the flight of steps led up to a lobby at first-floor level at the north end of the hall, which occupied the space over the three prison cells and the two rooms to the east of them, thus measuring about 48 by 28ft. The screens passage would be at the north end, where spiral stairs also led down to the basement, and the dais would be at the south end, lit by the bay window in the east wall. South of the hall lay the great chamber with a bay window to the south overlooking the river and another to the east probably serving as an oratory. Spiral stairs in the north-west angle of the chamber led down to the basement, and perhaps upwards to a bedchamber on the second floor. The thickness of the stair-block at the north end of the house suggests that a return flight led up from the lobby to the upper storey of the infirmary passage, serving as the abbot's gallery. Great breasts of masonry outside the north and south walls of the gallery represent fireplaces and a latrine, and the northern extension of the gallery led to the abbot's private pew looking into the Chapel of the Nine Altars. Off the west side of this northern gallery a room over the surviving basement of Abbot Huby's time was probably that known as the 'Church Chamber', used as the abbot's secretariat, with a latrine just south of it in the angle of the two galleries.

THE INFIRMARY

The infirmary was the part of the abbey where the sick and aged monks were housed and received treatment. It lay to the east of the other monastic buildings, insulated by them from the noise and bustle of the great court.

Although the abbey had an infirmary in the twelfth century, it was probably of timber and no remains of it survive. The low ruins of the present vast group of buildings mostly belong to the time of Abbot John of Kent (1220–47), and in order to gain room for them in the narrow valley he carried out a remarkably ambitious engineering scheme, canalizing the river into four parallel, stone vaulted tunnels over a distance of some 90yd to provide a level platform on which to build.

The central feature of this group is the great infirmary hall. East of it, from north to south, lie a two-storeyed block of chambers, a chapel, and yards enclosing a kitchen. West of it lie a small conduit house, the misericord or dining hall of the infirm monks, and other buildings now too extensively ruined to be identifiable. The group is linked to the cloister by a long passage.

The infirmary passage

The infirmary passage starts just south of the parlour and forms a gently inclined plane until it reaches the infirmary hall some 200ft to the east. About halfway along, a branch passage leads northwards to the Chapel of the Nine Altars. Only the lower walls of these passages remain, and they show many alterations.

Although there would be timber passages from the early days of the monastery, their replacement in stone did not start until the second quarter of the thirteenth century. The first passage to be built in stone was L-shaped, leading westwards from the infirmary hall for 90ft and then turning northwards to the Chapel of the Nine Altars. It was like a free-standing cloister alley, with open arcades on both sides in groups of three arches supported by twin shafts. At its west end a large archway on the south side led to a yard, and another archway to the west led to a timber continuation of the passage. Late in the thirteenth century this timber continuation was rebuilt in stone.

In the fourteenth century galleries of timber were built above these passages. To support them, the open arcades of the eastern and northern passages were blocked with masonry, and large masonry abutments were added outside the south wall of the east passage to support fire-places or bay windows in the galleries above. Late in the fifteenth century the galleries were again remodelled and made to serve the abbot's house. More masonry abutments for fireplace or bays, and two rectangular masonry shafts for latrines were added, as well as a small chamber off the west side of the northern passage. The basement of this chamber remains, with spiral stairs in one angle. Opposite it, in the east wall of the passage, there is a doorway to a yard and, just to the north, another rectangular platform of masonry near the gable of the Chapel of the Nine Altars. When first excavated in the nineteenth century, this platform was found to support remains of an oven, possibly for preparing the eucharistic wafers for the church.

The infirmary hall

At the eastern end of the passage lies the great hall of the infirmary, one of the largest halls in medieval Britain, measuring about 180 by 78ft and with an internal floor area of almost 12 000 sq ft. It straddles the river, with its long axis roughly from north to south. Only low walls remain, but they show that the hall had a central nave eight bays long and two bays wide, enclosed on both sides and at both ends with an aisle. The appearance of the piers supporting the vanished arcades can be seen from the example re-erected in the south-east corner from fragments found in the nineteenth-century excavations. Other fragments found at the same time show that the aisles once had twin lancet windows in each bay with a circular opening above, and that both nave and aisles were vaulted in stone at a uniform level, the nave having no clerestory. The hall was heated by fireplaces in the north and south aisles, and it may have had a central hearth as well.

When it was first built in the thirteenth century, the beds of the sick and aged monks would be ranged along the aisles, the central nave being left free. It soon became customary to screen the beds with curtains, in much the same way as a modern hospital ward, and from the fourteenth century onwards to replace the curtains with partitions of wood or stone, creating what were in effect small private wards in individual bays of the aisles. The nineteenth-century excavations revealed traces of this practice belonging to two different dates, but so flimsy that most of them no longer exist. In the fourteenth century most of the bays in the east aisle, and two towards the south end of the west aisle, were partitioned off as wards, and late in the fifteenth century the remaining bays of the west aisle were converted into rooms under Abbots Darnton and Huby. Five of the fireplaces serving these rooms remain, and twin latrine shafts outside the aisle walls towards the south. The base of a flight of steps found in the excavations showed that some of the rooms were in two storeys. In the west aisle the second and sixth bays from the north, and in the east aisle the third and sixth were left open as passages across the hall, linking the other buildings east and west of it.

The infirmary chambers

A building lies off the east side of the infirmary hall, near its northern end. It was built in the time of Abbot John of Kent and was two storeys high. The ground-floor room backs against the high platform carried by the tunnels, and so is some 8ft below the level of the infirmary hall, and the first floor was some 5ft above that level.

The ground-floor is well preserved, apart from its east wall which Aislabie replaced in the eighteenth century by a pair of rustic arches to give a more romantic aspect to the view from his belvedere at Anne Boleyn's Seat. The room was vaulted in five double bays from a central row of columns, and had a fireplace and a doorway in its north wall.

Little of the first-floor room survives, but access to it was by a flight of steps that once occupied the little sunken yard, originally open to the north, lying between it and the infirmary hall. This upper room communicated with a much ruined structure that overlapped its south-east angle and that certainly contained a privy and probably acted as a small inner chamber as well.

The original use of these rooms is not known. A similar two-storeyed block attached to the infirmary hall at the Cistercian abbey of Ours-camp in France about the same date had an apothecary's office and store on the ground floor and an isolation ward above, and it may be that these rooms at Fountains served some similar purpose.

Whatever their use, it was changed late in the thirteenth century, and alterations were made to them then and in the early fourteenth century. When the infirmary chapel was built against the south wall of the chamber block, access from it to the upper room was contrived by inserting a narrow flight of steps in the thickness of the wall shared by the two buildings. A second flight of steps outside the chapel's west wall led to a landing at the head of the stairs in the sunken courtyard, and the latrine annexe at the south-east angle of the upper room was shortened. The lower room was divided by cross walls into three small rooms, the easternmost reached by a narrow doorway and a breakneck flight of steps from outside the east end of the chapel, and the sunken court was provided with a new wall at the south end and a massive entrance arch to the north, showing that it and the stairs within it were now roofed.

At the end of the fifteenth century these stairs were abandoned. The arch on the north was blocked by a wall with a window in it, and the sunken court was floored at the level of the head of the former stairs, making a lobby outside the upper room. This lobby could now be reached by the stairs outside the west end of the chapel, and by a new flight rising from the east aisle of the infirmary hall. The upper room was also now provided with a private pew, the massive stone base of which remains, overlooking the chapel.

There is little doubt that these alterations represent the conversion of the block into lodgings for a retired abbot, for such apartments are often associated with infirmaries from the late thirteenth century onwards. Six abbots of Fountains resigned and lived on in retirement at the abbey, and the initial alterations to the block probably represent the creation of an establishment for the first of them, Abbot Peter Alyng, in 1279. At first this lodging had an independent entrance from the north, service stairs to the kitchen on the south, and private stairs by which the abbot could make use of the infirmary chapel. Later, when the creation of private rooms had robbed the infirmary hall of its communal use, the main entrance was moved to the west, and the ex-abbot could hear service from the private pew without descending into the chapel—both features reflecting increased status.

The infirmary chapel

The infirmary chapel was built against the south side of the chamber block late in the thirteenth century. It is a plain rectangle of two bays, separated from the infirmary hall by a small yard. Its west doorway gives on to this yard and is set north of centre to give room for a flight of steps to clear its head. Against the north wall of the chapel is the base of the pew belonging to the upper chamber, and just east of it the doorway to the narrow stairs leading up to that chamber. The pew was a late fifteenth-century addition, and once had a stone frieze and cornice carved with figures of a chained dragon and a monkey that are preserved in the museum. Part of the jamb of the group of lancets that formed the chapel's east window remains against the wall of the chamber block.

The infirmary kitchen

The infirmary kitchen lies to the south of the chapel and is separated from it and from the infirmary hall by small yards as a precaution against fire. A passage of irregular shape leads from the doorway in the kitchen's north wall to the yard between the chapel and the hall.

There would be an earlier kitchen on this site, replaced by the present stone building in the fourteenth century. It is a rectangular building divided by a cross-wall into a wide northern and narrow southern part, and its deep buttresses show that it was vaulted in stone.

The northern part was the main kitchen, with two doorways to the north and one to the west which led to a narrow annexe, now wholly ruined. The two kitchen fireplaces are in the cross-wall, and in the north-east angle of the room there is a great stone grid in the floor, forming part of the vault of the southernmost tunnel and looking like a mullioned and transomed window laid flat on the ground. This grid was once fitted with trap-doors and could be used for the disposal of kitchen waste directly into the river below. Late in the Middle Ages four ovens were built in the room; one was in the western annexe, the second in the cross-wall near the eastern fireplace, the third and largest projected through the east wall, and the fourth was set against that wall near the grid.

The southern part of the building was the scullery, reached by three doorways alternating with the two fireplaces in the cross-wall. There are remains of the flagged floor with its stone gutters and, when the second oven was made, a fireplace was built in this room against the back of the eastern fireplace in the main kitchen. There is a narrow recess in the east jamb of the westernmost doorway of the cross-wall, and when this was first excavated it was found to have contained a steep flight of stone steps, perhaps leading up into the flues where bacon could be hung for smoking.

The conduit house

The conduit house was built against the south wall of the infirmary passage, a little to the west of the infirmary hall, in the fourteenth century. It is a room of irregular shape, once paved with small stone flags. In the centre of the floor there was a space surrounded by a stone gutter, and the nineteenth-century excavations found a lead pipe leading from here under the floor towards the south. This pipe probably brought fresh water from the springs on Kitchen Bank down to a tank standing within the gutter, where a head of water could be built up and piped to the various parts of the abbey.

Late in the Middle Ages the room served other purposes and its western doorway was converted into a hatch. The early excavations uncovered quantities of kitchen refuse, broken pottery and ashes that had been shovelled through this hatch into the yard on the west, where a supply of coal was also found.

The misericord

The misericord projects at an angle from the south wall of the conduit house. It is a ground-floor hall, 58 by 22ft, and it may first have been built in the thirteenth century as a reredorter for the infirmary, for a row of seven latrine shafts exists along its south side, discharging into the tunnels.

Under Abbot Darnton, probably between 1489 and 1495, it was extensively remodelled and the latrine shafts were blocked. At this time it was being used as the misericord or dining hall where meat prepared in the infirmary kitchen was allowed to be eaten not only by the sick but also, from the fourteenth century, by the convent in general. The building is much ruined, but there are indications that it had a service passage at the east end with doorways leading south and east for kitchen service, and a dais remains at the west end, its step once faced with stones bearing a design of small quatrefoils. There are remains of a stone bench against the north wall.

Other buildings once existed south of the misericord, but they are completely ruined except for a fragment of their south wall with a small fireplace. Beyond them there was a walled yard against the south-west angle of the infirmary hall.

THE LAY-BROTHERS' INFIRMARY

This was built against the west end of the lay-brothers' reredorter towards the end of the twelfth century, and is carried over the river on four parallel vaulted tunnels. It was a great hall with aisles to east and west and with arcades of six bays on slender octagonal piers.

Only the north wall now stands to any height, with a central doorway and a well proportioned group of three windows above. The half-gable of the east aisle has an unusual quadrant window, and the outer walls of both aisles, now mostly gone, appear to have been built about two feet outside the ends of the tunnels and carried on arches springing from the cutwaters.

The general arrangements would be similar to those of the great hall of the monks' infirmary, with the sick beds in the aisles and the central nave used for the general services of the establishment. The east aisle may also have had wooden stairs up to the doorway in the west end of the lay-brothers' reredorter.

Another building, perhaps a kitchen, once stood outside the south-west angle of this infirmary hall.

The infirmary bridge

From the north-west angle of the lay-brothers' infirmary a high wall runs along the north bank of the river to the guest houses, and an archway in this wall leads to a bridge across the Skell. It was built in the twelfth century and is a rare survival, for few bridges of that date still exist in this country. Its three ribbed arches are separated by tri-angular cutwaters both upstream and downstream. Its parapets are of later date.

THE GUEST HOUSES

These stand in what was once a walled courtyard occupying the bend of the river west of the lay-brothers' infirmary. There are substantial remains of two of them, both built shortly after the middle of the twelfth century, and they are amongst the best examples in Britain of a particular type of stone dwelling house that is also found in towns, on manors, and as domestic accommodation within castles during the twelfth and thirteenth centuries. Each is a simple rectangular building of two storeys, with a hall, chamber, and privy on each floor. In the twelfth century, therefore, they were capable of providing four complete and independent sets of accommodation for important visitors and their travelling households.

The east guest house

The east guest house is the better preserved of the two. As first built, its ground floor was entered by a doorway in the north wall and was vaulted in six double bays from a central row of elaborate clustered piers. It was divided into two rooms, each of three bays, as can be seen from the change in the design of the piers and from the slightly greater width of the windows in the northern half, which formed the lower hall. The southern half was the lower chamber, from the south-west angle of which a doorway leads to a privy in a turret projecting into the bed of the river. Another doorway led to a timber balcony bracketed out over the river between the turret and the infirmary bridge.

Most of the upper storey has gone. It was reached by external stairs against the west wall of the building. The upper hall was four bays long, with a fireplace in its east wall and a group of two two-light windows and a circular window above in the north gable. The upper chamber had a window to the south and a doorway to a privy in the upper storey of the turret.

Later in the Middle Ages the arrangements were altered. A cross-wall was inserted dividing the ground floor into two rooms of four and two bays, the north doorway was converted into a window and a new doorway was made at the north end of the west wall, the lower chamber was given an external doorway of its own by breaking through a window in its west wall, and the external stairs were provided with a masonry base containing two tiny rooms or closets. On the upper floor a fireplace was put between the two windows in the north gable, and the circular window above was blocked to take its flue. Its stone chimney remains complete on the apex of the gable.

The west guest house

The west guest house is similar but smaller, being of four double bays. In the twelfth century a doorway at the east end of the house led into the lower hall, probably of two bays, which had a fireplace on the south and was separated by a partition from the lower chamber. This was also of two bays, with a doorway to a privy in a turret over the river at the south-west angle of the building. At this date the external stairs to the first floor may have been against the north wall.

The upper storey is too much ruined for its arrangements to be recovered with certainty, but the upper hall fireplace remains in the south wall and has a lamp bracket and part of a boldly projecting stone hood. The upper chamber had access to a privy in the turret, and its west wall had two windows with a circular window above in the gable.

In the thirteenth century a wing as large as the original building was added to its north side. Little of this remains but excavation showed that it had a large chimney breast in its north wall. The upper chamber was also provided with a fireplace in its west wall, the flue of which blocked the circular window.

More extensive alterations were made in the fourteenth century, and can best be appreciated by reference to the plan. They included the buttressing and perhaps the vaulting of the added wing, and the provision of new external stairs and a curved passage at the junction of the wing and the house. They were perhaps connected with the use of the wing as a kitchen, and the conversion of the end bay of the west house into a 'screens' passage serving both floors of both houses. A bridge probably linked the head of the new stairs with the stair block of the east house. The angle between the two guest houses was also walled in and provided with a fireplace, forming a small chamber that probably served as an office for the guest master.

Ambitious as they are, these surviving guest houses only formed part of a larger group. Excavation showed that other buildings had stood to the north-west, extending as far as the river bank where a pair of massive corbels for a latrine remains in the river wall.

THE PRECINCT AND ITS BUILDINGS

The church and the main buildings of the abbey stood near the centre of a precinct that enclosed Skelldale over a distance of rather more than half a mile and covered an area of about 70 acres. The quarried face of the rocks formed a sufficient boundary on most of the north side, which was also covered by the abbey's grange at Swanley on top of Rye Bank overlooking the dale. On the other sides the precinct was enclosed by a stone wall, some 12ft high to the top of its coping. Much of this wall remains to its full height along the south boundary, outside the Department's guardianship, and its foundations can also be seen crossing the valley about 500yd east of the abbey buildings. Outside the precinct to the south lay the abbey's grange of Morker, and to the south-west was Fountains Park with its extensive fishponds.

Within this main boundary the precinct was subdivided into lesser areas and courtyards for different purposes. The main division was the River Skell running from west to east through the whole precinct and canalized within stone banks for much of its length. North of the river there is a fairly level but narrow tract of land, no more than 25yd wide at the west end but increasing to 150yd wide in the centre of the dale. Along this strip lay the main courtyards and buildings of the abbey. South of the river a much wider but undulating area was given over to the agricultural and industrial activities necessary for provisioning the abbey and working its estates. There were eastern, southern, and western gates to the precinct, but the position of only the last is known.

The outer court

The main entrance to the precinct was from the west, at the point where the visitor today leaves the Aldfield road to enter the grounds. Here stood the west gates, of which there are no remains. They led to a narrow court—almost a corridor—flanked on the south by the river and on the north by a high wall, part of the eastern end of which remains and shows traces where sheds for carts stood against it.

This court was the abbey's main link with the outside world and it contained a number of buildings, but its arrangements were mostly destroyed by the building of Fountains Hall. One of the buildings was the Chapel of St Mary at the Gates, for the use of layfolk and especially of women, who were not admitted farther into the precinct except on special occasions. Another was the hospice or lay-infirmary where rudimentary medical treatment was given to the poor. It had its own endowments, even including one to provide veils for the heads of those being treated for ringworm. It was a very considerable establishment, which included the services of the almonry where charity was dispensed to the poor, a common dormitory or 'casual ward' for tramps and other poor travellers, and chambers for aged pensioners.

In the later Middle Ages, although a monk-porter was still nominally in charge of the hospice and the west gates, the actual work was done by a lay porter and his wife who doubled as laundress to the abbot. They had their own cottage and land for a stable in the court.

The only medieval building now remaining in the court is a ruin

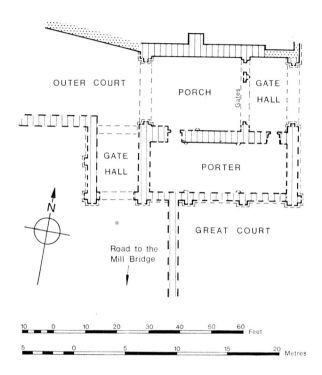

OUTER COURT

PORCH

Gates

GATE

HALL

GATE

HALL

PORTER

N

GREAT COURT

Road to the
Mill Bridge

| 10 | 0 | 10 | 20 | 30 | 40 | 50 | 60 | Feet |

| 5 | 0 | 5 | 10 | 15 | 20 | Metres |

tucked into the slope just east of the nineteenth-century west lodge. It is of twelfth-century date and may have formed part of the hospice.

The gatehouse and the great court

The eastern end of the outer court was closed by the gatehouse which gave access to the great court in front of the abbey buildings.

The gatehouse was built early in the thirteenth century, and its arrangements are best understood by reference to the plan, for the lower parts of its walls are buried and the only remains now visible are the upper parts of the north and south walls of the gate passage. This passage was once entered by a wide western archway and it was vaulted throughout. The western part formed a covered lobby or porch outside the gates, which were hung within the passage. There was a large gate for carts and a smaller doorway for pedestrians, and beyond them a short hall with an eastern arch into the great court. The south side of the gate passage was covered by an equally long and narrow building. It had doorways into the passage both in front of and behind the gates, and it was the porter's lodge, giving him access to visitors waiting in the porch for the main gates to be opened. There was also a doorway on the north side of the passage, behind the gates, that probably led to stairs to an upper floor.

Projecting from the west end of the porter's lodge and forming part of the structure of the gatehouse there was a smaller gate passage through the south wall of the outer court. This led by way of the mill bridge to the southern parts of the precinct beyond the river.

The cemetery and the eastern precinct

The cemetery lay beyond the east end of the Chapel of the Nine Altars. It was thoroughly ransacked after the dissolution, and only a few grave covers remain.

Beyond the cemetery, the eastern parts of the precinct north of the river were taken up by orchards and gardens.

The southern precinct and its buildings

The steep southern slope of the valley opposite the abbey buildings was wooded in the Middle Ages, as it is now, and was known as Kitchen Bank. Beyond it, on the brow of the hill, there was an enclosure called Pondgarth from the group of fishponds it contained. There is a smaller fishpond farther to the west. Pondgarth was enclosed by 8 acres of orchard known as East Applegarth, and west of this were three more orchards, amounting to 12 acres, called the West Applegarths.

The main agricultural and industrial buildings of the abbey lay in this part of the precinct, south of the river, but the sites of most of them are not known. They included the barns, the tannery, the wool house, the cheese house, the mills, the malthouse, the bakehouse, the carpenter's shop, the wheelwright's shop, the smithy, and many more. Only the mills and the combined malthouse and bakehouse survive. They were reached by a road which left the outer court through the small gate passage at the west end of the gatehouse.

The mill bridge

This road crossed the Skell by a fine early thirteenth-century bridge of two arches which remains complete. The northern arch took the flow of the Skell and of one of the two leats that fed the mill. The southern arch took the outfall of the second leat, now blocked.

The mill

The mill was fed by a leat drawn from the Skell just outside the west wall of the precinct and led parallel to that river and some 20yd south of it to a point about 100yd south west of the gatehouse, where it widened into a millpond straddled by the abbey mill. The mill (or mills, for there were two water-wheels and two cornmills under one roof) is a remarkable building that remained in use from the twelfth to the early part of the twentieth century. Although the north end was demolished after the dissolution and partly replaced by lower structures, the medieval building still stands to a length of 110ft. It was first built before the middle of the twelfth century, and was remodelled later in that century and early in the thirteenth century. It is not at present open to visitors.

The bakehouse

The bakehouse is much ruined and overgrown. It lies on the south bank of the Skell opposite the guest houses, and it was built in the first half of the thirteenth century but made use of the thick north and south walls of an earlier twelfth-century building on the same site.

Few of its arrangements can be made out today, but originally there was a stone-paved passage at the south end, with a doorway and a fireplace. A narrow room lay north of this, its centre taken up with a battery of two or possibly three ovens. To the west of the ovens there was a semicircular stone recess with a groove for a waterpipe, and in front of it a large stone trough. This was perhaps a kneading place for dough, and there are traces of another one farther west where the outer wall of the building projects to house it. North of the ovens was a larger room, and the east side of the whole building was covered by a pentise.

Plan 3   The Bakehouse and Malthouse

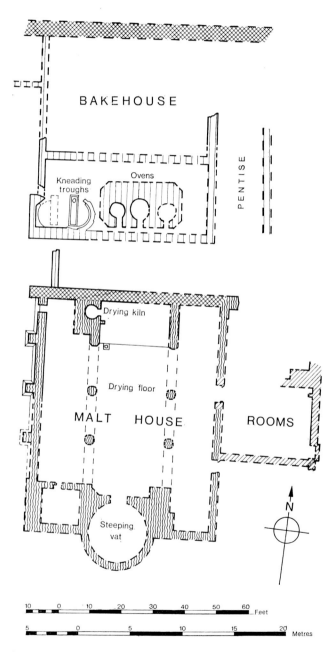

BAKEHOUSE

PENTISE

Kneading troughs

Ovens

Drying kiln

Drying floor

MALT HOUSE

ROOMS

Steeping vat

N

| 10 | 0 | 10 | 20 | 30 | 40 | 50 | 60 | Feet |

| 5 | 0 | 5 | 10 | 15 | 20 | Metres |

The malthouse

The malthouse backs on to the south wall of the bakehouse and is also much ruined. It was built in the second half of the thirteenth century as an aisled hall with deep responds at each end and two pairs of piers between. The north-west respond had a circular hearth or kiln with a breast projecting into the west aisle. The central part of the building had a slightly raised stone floor with a circular drain at its north-west angle. In the south part of the building, the end of the west aisle was walled off to form a small room, and the central nave was filled by a great circular vat of cemented brick.

This vat would be for steeping and draining the barley, the raised platform in the centre of the floor would be for drying, and the kiln at the north-west angle would be for a final drying of the malt under heat. The building had an upper storey, probably used for brewing, as chases for waterpipes descend from it.

Another building was added to the east side of the malthouse in the fourteenth century, with a fireplace in the south-east angle and a privy in the north-east angle. It may have been of two storeys, serving as chambers and offices for the two obedientiaries who had charge of the building—the monk of the bakery and the monk of the brewery.

CONVERSION TABLE

1ft	0.3m	30yd	27·4m
5ft	1·5m	35yd	32·0m
10ft	3·0m	40yd	36·6m
15ft	4·6m	45yd	41·1m
20ft	6·1m	50yd	45·7m
25ft	7·6m	100yd	91·4m
30ft	9·1m	200yd	182·9m
35ft	10·7m	300yd	274·3m
40ft	12·2m	400yd	365·8m
45ft	13·7m	500yd	457·2m
50ft	15·2m	1000yd	914·4m
100ft	30·5m		
		1 acre	0·40ha
1yd	0·9m	5 acres	2·02ha
5yd	4·6m	10 acres	4·05ha
10yd	9·1m		
15yd	13·7m	1 mile	1·60km
20yd	18·3m	5 miles	8·04km
25yd	22·9m	10 miles	16·09km

Short Bibliography

History

J. R. Walbran: Memorials of the Abbey of St. Mary of Fountains (Surtees Society Publications, vol. xlii; 1863)

W. Dugdale: Monasticon Anglicanum, vol. v, 292–306 (1817–30)

W. T. Lancaster: Fountains Chartulary (1915)

J. Burton: Monasticon Eboracense (1758)

Victoria County History, Yorkshire, vol. iii, 134–8 (1913)

L. G. D. Baker: The Foundation of Fountains Abbey (Northern History, vol. iv, 29–43; 1969)

E. F. Jacob: A disputed election at Fountains Abbey (Medieval Studies presented to Rose Graham; 78–97; 1950)

C. H. Talbot: Letters from the English Abbots to the Chapter at Cîteaux (Camden Society, 4th series, vol. iv; 1967)

Excavations and buildings

J. R. Walbran's papers on the nineteenth-century excavations are collected in Surtees Society Publications, vol. lxvii (1876)

W. H. St. J. Hope: Fountains Abbey (Yorkshire Archaeological Journal, vol. xv, 269–402; 1900)

J. A. Reeve: Monograph on the Abbey of St. Mary of Fountains (1892)

A. W. Oxford: The Ruins of Fountains Abbey (1910 and many later editions)

R. Gilyard-Beer: Fountains Abbey, the early buildings 1132–50 (Archaeological Journal, vol cxxv, 313–9; 1969)

Glossary

ALMONRY	Building or room from which alms were given to the poor and sick.
AUMBRY	Cupboard or recess in the thickness of a wall.
BUTTRESS	Masonry (or brickwork) built against a wall for additional strength.
CELLARER	Monastic official in charge of provisioning the monastery.
CHAPTER HOUSE	The room in which the monks met daily for monastic business when an article or chapter (capitulum) of the monastic rule was read.
CLERESTORY	Upper storey of the nave whose windows admitted light to the central part of the church.
CORBEL	Stone bracket projecting from a wall.
DAY STAIRS	Daytime access from the dormitory to the cloister.
DORTER	Dormitory.
FRATER	Refectory or dining hall.
GARTH	Area enclosed by the cloister.
HOODMOULD	Weathering or drip-stone protecting the head of door or window.
LANCET	Narrow window with a pointed head.
LAVER	Trough with running water where monks washed their hands before meals.
LAY BRETHREN	Monks not in Holy Orders who performed manual labour.
MISERICORD	Room in a monastery where it was permitted to eat meat.
NIGHT STAIRS	Access from the dormitory direct into the church, used by monks for night offices.
PARLOUR	Room in which conversation was allowed.
PENTISE	A penthouse or lean-to, often used as a passage.
PISCINA	Small basin in a wall beside an altar, used for cleansing the sacramental vessels.
PRESBYTERY	Part of the eastern arm of the church containing the principal altar and reserved for the clergy.
PULPITUM	Partition between nave and choir.
REBUS	A representation of a name or word by pictures.
REREDORTER	Building containing latrines, usually flushed by a channel of running water.
REREDOS	Ornamental screen behind an altar.
RESPOND	Half-column or half-capital, attached to a wall where it is joined by an arch.
ROOD SCREEN	Division between nave and choir west of the pulpitum and surmounted by a crucifix.
SACRISTY	Place for keeping the sacred vessels and vestments.
SPRINGER	Lowest stone of an arch or vaulting rib.
STOUP	Basin.
STRING COURSE	Horizontal band of masonry.
TRIFORIUM	Wall passage between the main arcade and clerestory.
UNDERCROFT	Chamber, usually vaulted, supporting a principal chamber above.
VILL	A territorial division under feudal system.
WARMING HOUSE	Room in a monastery where a communal fire was kept burning during the winter months.

Printed in Scotland by Her Majesty's Stationery Office at HMSO Press, Edinburgh
Dd 586449 K338 7/78 (15118)